# CRYPTO CRAZE

## BITCOIN - STANDARD HARD MONEY OF THE FUTURE - BEGINNERS GUIDE TO CRYPTOCURRENCIES AND BLOCKCHAIN BASICS

## C.D. KING

# CONTENTS

# INTRODUCTION

Crypto craze stands for the predominant kind of emotion that have surrounded cryptocurrencies thus far. But, how do cryptocurrencies actually work? How is one supposed to buy them and sell them? What is crypto investing and how different is it from regular mainstream investing? Why do people say crypto is like money, but that it has revolutionized the way money works?

In other words, besides the rush and the curiosity, there are simply too many unknowns around crypto. It is challenging on a technological level and also on a financial level, so it seems to go against the very first rule of good investors: that you should never put your money on something you don't understand.

But you're aware of the potential benefits. That's why you're here. So how should you go about learning about crypto and making it an investment you do understand?

Throughout this book, I will give you all the basics and give you a detailed explanation of some of the most technically challenging aspects. I will give you examples, elaborations on what each thing means in the context of regular finance, and I will give you my personal opinion too. Armed with these tools, you will be able to handle yourself with confidence while sailing the uncharted waters of the cryptoverse.

Even then, your learning process must continue. Think of this book as a door that will open a new financial world before your eyes, but not as a final stop at all. I don't intend to give you all the answers, but rather to show you the know-how you need to keep learning on your own indefinitely.

Bitcoin is the first attempt at a currency that uses the blockchain technology to have a global, decentralized, peer-to-peer payment network. It is such a radical innovation that, since 2008, it has inspired the creation of many more cryptocurrencies. The amount of people using crypto is so big nowadays that you simply cannot afford to keep ignoring it any longer. You should be very careful about how you get into that world, but under no circumstance should you give up on this great opportunity.

So how about you mix some of that crypto craze with some solid crypto know-how? I guarantee that the moment you do this, everything you know about finance will change completely. There are a variety of ways for you to use crypto as an investment and collect much higher returns than those of most traditional investments. You just need to commit, work hard and think clearly at every step of the way. The rest will come on its own.

Since at least 2017, crypto has been in the limelight. It no longer sits on a college shelf, like a student's idea written on a white paper, but never implemented. Neither does it sit relegated at the outskirts of the world economy. It is still certainly a small asset class with a modest market cap. Yet the potential for growth is there. It has already shown its face a number of times in the past.

If you too want to embark on this huge novelty of the 21st century, you must first of all get rid of the FOMO attitude most others adopt. Forget what others told you about becoming rich overnight with crypto. There are those who will indulge in that illusion to sell you a thing or two, but the reality is quite different. For all its incredible feats, crypto is no fairy tale. It is a new, highly demanding, highly complex asset class that even the most well learned don't understand in depth. So treat it with respect and be very cautious about your every move around crypto. I will teach you how to take advantage of it, but only you can use these tips and lessons in the right way.

Ideally, you should end this book with an urge for more information. This is the start of a lifelong interest that should go beside you from this point on. Crypto is still very new, so you will have to update what you learn about it almost every single day. So let's get started on this! Join me and I will teach you how to turn your crypto craze into crypto wealth.

# CHAPTER 1
# WHAT IS BITCOIN?

You certainly know the word and have some general idea about it not being a simple thing. In a way, that is why you got this book: to find answers as to what Bitcoin is beyond mere greetings and a good afternoon. You want to know more; you might even be pondering inside your head whether it could be a good investment. Not right now, of course, but later, after you get to know it better.

Well, good news. Bitcoin can indeed be a great investment, but you're right. It's not a good idea to get into it without understanding it first. By now, this has pretty much come to be a universal rule of investing: don't put your money into something you don't understand. So let's understand. Let's have a closer look at Bitcoin and crypto in general and let us begin by stating the information of rigor.

## A BRIEF BACKGROUND

Bitcoin is the first cryptocurrency to be created. The term cryptocurrency itself is a combination of the two main ingredients in it, a form of digital money that works on the basis of cryptography. Bitcoin was invented at some point around the early 2000s and it was first released in August 2009. A little later, in May 2010, one Laszlo

Hanyecz performed the first real commercial transaction by purchasing two pizzas for the 2010 value of 10 thousand Bitcoin.

At the current value of Bitcoin, that amount would be equivalent today to around 600 million dollars. That means the people who let go of their Bitcoin too easily during the first period of its existence must probably feel a bit regretful. In purchasing things with Bitcoin back when it was worth less than 1% of its current value, they effectively gave away their future fortune. Then again, who could have known at the time?

Those who were familiar with the project might have had some clue. In terms of timing, Bitcoin's creation coincides with the advent of the 2008 subprime financial crisis. This is in fact mentioned in the first transaction ever performed with Bitcoin, dated August 1st, 2009. The record of this transaction contains a newspaper headline from January 3, 2009 that reads: "Chancellor on brink of second bailout for banks."

This little detail has been interpreted as a sign of the spirit in which Bitcoin was created. To this day, it is widely regarded as a sort of angered manifestation against dysfunctions in the modern financial system, and also as a potential alternative to it. However, much of this cannot go too far beyond speculation. This is because there are various unanswerable questions about Bitcoin's origin. Several features about how it works make it pretty clear that it was intended to question and perhaps even enhance the way we think about money in the 21st century. That being said, the fact is Bitcoin has come a long way since it was first introduced, but one thing it hasn't yet accomplished is being used as money. People actually use it to invest, trying to take advantage of the huge upshifts in price it is known for. But afterwards, they all tend to get off the wagon pretty soon in order to avoid losses. Why is that? Why don't they trust Bitcoin beyond having won at blackjack?

Here's the thing. The way Bitcoin is supposed to change modern money is by getting rid of two qualities any typical form of money has. One of them is the presence of a regulating entity, normally a central bank, and the other is inflation. Both these changes make Bitcoin an unregulated, highly volatile asset. Moreover, they are hardcoded in the actual blueprint for Bitcoin, which is an open source piece of software, available for free download on the bitcoin.org website. This software is run by those who are in charge of processing transactions, also known as miners, but we'll actually talk more about them in the next chapter.

The Bitcoin network is kept alive by all of those who have the Bitcoin software up and running on a computer. Each of them has the entire history of transactions in their memory drives, which means the network doesn't rely on a central server, but rather on data that is repeatedly stored across a whole bunch of computers. Thus this system is based on repetition and it makes it possible to dispense with any form of central management unit. Instead, it runs itself. All it asks for in return is that it be stored in as many computers as possible.

That's how Bitcoin manages to be decentralized. As for inflation, the software also prohibits that there ever be more than a total of 21 million Bitcoin in circulation. This is actually not the current supply, it's a number we're supposed to reach somewhere around the year 2100. The more transactions there are, the more it takes for new Bitcoin to be created, which causes the cryptocurrency to have a supply that slows down the closer it gets to the limit.

Together, these are arguably the two main qualities of Bitcoin: the fact that it doesn't have a regulating authority other than its own rules, and the fact that its total supply is capped at 21 million. For those of you who aren't even familiar with money in general, these qualities might sound rather mundane. However, the fact is they're so radically new that, in little more than a decade, they have totally revolutionized the world of money, exactly as expected.

There's a whole bunch of more technical stuff around the Bitcoin software, things that only computer geeks can grasp. For those who look at Bitcoin strictly as an investment, though, the problem is not much more can be deduced from its technical details. We know the people who created it didn't like central banks or inflation very much and we know they also didn't think much about the logistical implications. By this I'm referring to the sheer amount of electricity consumption Bitcoin requires to be functional.

In reality, no one can make a precise calculation of how much energy Bitcoin uses, precisely because it is decentralized, but the ballpark itself is pretty enormous. According to the Bitcoin Energy Consumption Index, offered and updated regularly by Alex de Vries on Digiconomist, Bitcoin currently represents an electricity expenditure of just under 200 TWh every year. This is a consumption comparable to that of a well sized industrial country, such as Thailand, France or the UK.

All in all, Bitcoin is an invention that has undoubtedly proven to be revolutionary, but still has big unknowns awaiting in the future. It is currently used as an investment asset rather than a means of payment. Then again, that's actually good news for us because it means there are a variety of ways in which we can hop on the Bitcoin wagon and make the most of it. We just need to be careful what we get into and double check every step we take. The reality is Bitcoin's full story has yet to unravel completely. That means financial predictions surrounding it shouldn't be taken as truth.

## WHO CREATED BITCOIN?

The first unknown, still unanswered to this day, is the question of who actually invented Bitcoin. No one knows for sure. There is only a pseudonym at the center of it all, Satoshi Nakamoto, but it is uncertain whether it's a real name or whether it belongs to a single person. Over the years there have been a number of theories about it and even some attempts to locate the person behind the name, but they've all resulted in flops. At least for now, the truth is we don't know who Satoshi Nakamoto really is, so all we will say here about him, give or take, you will certainly find mentioned elsewhere.

Satoshi released technical details on a mailing list about the original Bitcoin project, back when it was still in its infancy. During this process they also exchanged ideas back and forth with other computer programmers. The product of this work was a now world famous white paper in which all the specifications about what Bitcoin is, how it works, what changes it brings to the table, etc. It's an academic type paper, so it's not intended to be friendly with the popular audience. Still, if you really want to dig into it, you can find it at bitcoin.org and download it for free.

After the publication of the Bitcoin white paper, Satoshi went completely silent. This of course added to the mystery to the point it almost sounds like science fiction stuff. And things keep going from there. There are several people who have been approached by the press because they were thought to be Satoshi. Others have gone public holding similar claims of their own. In 2014, an article came out in *Newsweek* (McGrath, 2014) claiming to unveil the mysterious identity of Bitcoin's creator. The author of the article had tracked and found a Japanese-American man living in California, who apparently fit the profile on account of being a mathematician and a loner. He was in his 60s and his real name was Dorian Satoshi Nakamoto. This version was quickly debunked, initially because the man denied being the real Satoshi, but also because no conclusive evidence was found to prove him wrong.

Just months after this event, another journalist published an article in *Forbes* magazine (Greenberg, 2014) saying a man who was no doubt involved in Bitcoin's early stages turned out to be living just a few blocks away from the one Dorian Satoshi Nakamoto that had just been outed in the *Newsweek* article. The man's name was Hal Finney and the article built an argument around a writing style test, reportedly proving that Finney's style resembled Satoshi's to the point of where it was possible to assert they were the same person. This version was also discredited because after approaching Finney, the author of the article concluded he was very close to the Bitcoin project, but was likely not the inventor himself.

A year later, in 2015, *Wired* (Branwen, 2015) and *Gizmodo* (Biddle and Cush, 2015) reported having been approached out of the blue by a hacker with evidence pointing to a man, one Craig Wright, who could be the real Satoshi. They were careful not to make any categorical statements, but still made a case for why it could be reasonable to believe him. In this case, many among the Bitcoin community remained incredulous, probably on the basis of the two previously disproved suspects. However, by 2016 Wright himself had assumed he was the real identity behind Satoshi. Many more news outlets interviewed him and concluded he was in fact a very well learned man, but that there was no real evidence connecting him to Bitcoin's creation.

But the first major suspect of this kind was actually Nick Szabo, a cryptography expert who had also published an early paper describing a system almost identical to that of Bitcoin. This man was outed in a 2013 blog post (Biggs, 2013) as possibly the real Satoshi, but no further evidence was ever produced beyond pointing out he, like Finney before, was aware of the project during its early stages and also shared the enthusiasm. Besides him, there have been a number of other minor suspects, but not much more. There is simply no solid evidence pointing to Satoshi's identity anywhere, except for one single detail: Satoshi's Bitcoin address.

This is the thing. As I said, there can only ever be 21 million Bitcoin in circulation. Now, since the Bitcoin software is open source, this rule is technically not written in stone. Judging by the predominant consensus, however, it seems unlikely that it will ever be changed. Because of this, a single unit of Bitcoin is much more valuable than, say, one dollar. I know talking about this subject, you may be thinking of Bitcoin's current value, but that's not exactly what I mean. Instead, I'm referring to a rule of economics that goes a little something like this: when a currency has a limited supply, having a large amount of it can have big effects on the value of the outstanding circulation. In other words, if the total pool of money in existence were one thousand dollars, then having a one hundred dollar bill is a very big deal.

What am I getting at with this? Well, whoever Satoshi is, the fact is their Bitcoin address, their account if you will, currently holds one million Bitcoin. We know this because Satoshi's address is recorded in the first transaction; we also know this address has been totally inactive since then. This is a pretty big deal because it means that, at the current value of Bitcoin, Satoshi holds a fortune worth 60 billion dollars. Moreover, it means Satoshi has the power to significantly change the outstanding amount of Bitcoin in circulation, thereby affecting its price as well.

In reality, nowadays there are several regulations around large Bitcoin transactions. In other words, whoever Satoshi is, they would have to go through a lot of scrutiny before they were able to actually spend any major amount of Bitcoin. Still, the fact Satoshi holds so much of the final supply has led people to think it is preferable if Satoshi remains anonymous indefinitely. Now, I know the mystery is pretty attractive, but my advice would be: don't fall for sensationalist news reports that claim to have found who Satoshi really is. They are often deceitful and can even lead to scams. Our ultimate goal is to make money with Bitcoin, and that requires us to stay away from risk.

## HOW DO ALTCOINS GET CREATED?

Decentralization has its virtues. One of them, no doubt, is the fact that anyone is free to use the original Bitcoin software, run it as is or tweak it if they want to, and launch their very own cryptocurrency. The product of this endeavor is what we now call an "altcoin," an alternative cryptocurrency other than Bitcoin.

Creating an altcoin is not so much an option for people who aren't computer savvy, but it's far more accessible than anyone would think. All that is stopping you from doing it is the work that it takes.

The downside, however, is pretty obvious. With no regulating center of any kind, either for one cryptocurrency or all of them combined, notoriety is tough to achieve. You're basically at the mercy of popular whim, trends and chance.

This has meant that although there are currently some fourteen thousand cryptocurrencies in circulation (Frankenfield, 2021), only a handful of them are widely known and used. Moreover, none of them is still trusted as a totally reliable store of value, meaning cryptocurrencies aren't thought of as money quite yet. Instead, each well-known altcoin has developed a sort of reputation for being especially good at something. In other words, every altcoin has a specialty. Some of them make crypto mining less expensive now that Bitcoin mining has become so competitive and expensive for independent miners. Others are designed to protect your identity in a variety of ways besides Bitcoin's original layout for anonymity. Others still, are linked to the price of a non-crypto asset, such as regular fiat money or some precious commodity, to hold a stable value. Depending on which of these you're looking at, we have three broad types of altcoins:

- Proof of Work (PoW) and Proof of Stake (PoS) altcoins

All mining based cryptocurrencies use either a PoW or PoS verification system. We will get into this in the next chapter, but it's basically a computational requirement for the network to allow new transactions to be validated. Because of this, mining has been increasingly done in the form of an arms race of tech gear, using more and more specialized computers for the purpose. These specialized computers are known as ASICs and they can be rather costly. Fortunately, some altcoins, such as Ethereum or Litecoin, can still be mined with cheaper domestic GPUs.

- Privacy coins

These altcoins, for example Monero, ZCash or PirateCoin, claim that Bitcoin's anonymous public/private key system doesn't really protect your identity. Because they take privacy a step further, they have been criticized for potentially being a cloaking tool for money laundering and criminal activity. However, their typical comeback to this kind of criticism is pretty solid: they also offer protection to political activists.

The way they work is they give you additional ephemeral account numbers besides your real ones. In this way, both the sender and receiver of a transaction can exchange crypto without actually changing their real account information. Moreover, anyone who intercepts the transaction midway can only trace ephemeral numbers that lead nowhere.

- Stablecoins

The lack of a regulating authority gives you freedom, but it also means the price of an asset is more likely to have sudden changes. Stablecoins are meant to address this very problem, which is called volatility. To prevent this from happening to them, stablecoins are linked to a reserve asset. This has two implications for us: 1) mining doesn't apply to them, and 2) they are cryptocurrencies, but ultimately they're denominated in a different asset class. They can be linked to the price of gold or the US dollar, for example. They do this by having a slightly more centralized management that is in charge of tracking the value of the reserve asset. Some popular examples are Tether, Binance USD or USD Coin, and you can use them to switch back and forth with other cryptocurrencies at a lower price than the one you'd have to pay by exchanging your crypto for fiat currency.

———

Although Bitcoin was the first cryptocurrency ever to be created, we now live in a world that has thousands of them. Later on, we will also learn about a new centralized form of cryptocurrencies that governments have been working on at least since 2019. However, our concern is with decentralized crypto alone. Throughout this book, whenever we address other forms of money, like fiat currency or government cryptocurrencies, we'll do it in the interest of knowing the competition.

At the heart of it all, crypto implies a new concept of public money that didn't exist before. As you will learn when we reach the last chapter, it is still uncertain what will happen to it in the end. But one thing we can all rely on is that crypto's contributions will remain in place one way or another.

## CHAPTER SUMMARY

- Bitcoin is nowadays in everybody's radar primarily because of its huge rise in price. It is seen as an investment rather than as a currency.
- Bitcoin's creation was arguably inspired by the 2008 financial crisis, as a kind of response to the dysfunctionalities of the modern economy.
- Bitcoin is unique in that it has a supply limit at 21 million. This leads to it being scarce and deflationary, as opposed to all other forms of fiat currency.
- Bitcoin is a combination of highly advanced information theory applications, cryptography and economics. Whoever wishes to learn about it must be prepared for a healthy dose of technical stuff.
- The pseudonym that sits behind Bitcoin, Satoshi Nakamoto, is still unknown today. No one knows the real identity of Bitcoin's creator.
- There have been several candidates over the years, people who were thought to be the real Satoshi, but nothing conclusive as of now.
- The original Bitcoin software is free and open source, which is how all other cryptocurrencies, so-called altcoins, have been developed.
- Altcoins can be grouped according to their specific applications, the three most prominent being those that are mined, those aimed at extra privacy, and those pegged to an underlying asset, also known as stablecoins.
- There is also such a thing as government issued cryptocurrencies nowadays, at least as a blueprint project. These are not our concern in this book, but it's worth saying they're crypto's biggest contender.

# CHAPTER 2
# WHAT IS BLOCKCHAIN?

This is going to be the most technical chapter. It's important to have it, even if our primary focus is crypto investment, because crypto is a technological invention and only by appreciating it in that sense will we be able to take full advantage of it.

The fundamental idea is as follows. Cryptocurrency, as I said in the beginning, is actually a combination of two things, cryptography and digital money. In other words, it's a system to code and decode information, except in this case the information are transactions between people. The way both these aspects get combined is called the blockchain. The blockchain is a form of database that, on its own, is arguably enough of an innovation for making Satoshi a bit of a Nobel Prize candidate. It can be the foundation for all sorts of applications, not just money. The reason it is so great is that it's a very ingenious way to keep information safe without the need for a centralized storage system.

To get a grasp of this, a good way is looking at the internet and how we interact with it. Let's say you're holding your phone as you normally would and you type a word in your browser. This input is sent by your device to a server, which in turn causes the server to respond to it by sending information to your phone. In other words, you type in the word cat, and you get a list of cat related links in return. All this information isn't really stored on your phone, but you're able to access it because you're connected to the server that does.

Now, what would happen if that server went down for some reason? Better still, what would happen if we had an outage like that Facebook earlier this year? (Janardhan, 2021). In such a case, our problem would be that a central server located somewhere in the planet has ceased to broadcast its "home address," if you will. Of course, other computers around the world would now be unable to find their way to the server, causing the whole network to go still, almost dead. This is basically what happened during Facebook's outage, proving once again that even state of the art networks suffer from a basic design flaw.

What is that flaw? It's simple: they all rely on a central unit where all their information is stored. Of course they have security copies and whatnot, but nothing that comes close to the resilience provided by a blockchain type database. In the latter case, innumerable copies of the same information are being made all the time, each with every new user that joins the network (miners, in the case of crypto). That way information is repeated enough times that losing a single storage unit doesn't represent an existential damage to it. For a blockchain database to stop working, it would be necessary to take down every computer on its network, or at least a big percentage of them, and that's just next to impossible.

## HOW IT DIFFERS FROM REGULAR BANKING

When applied to digital money, the blockchain technology takes the form of an open ledger. The word ledger comes from accounting practice and it refers to a sheet where all transactions are recorded. So what we have in the Bitcoin blockchain is a long list of transactions where every entry specifies the sender, the receiver and the amount being exchanged. This entry then goes to the bottom of the list, along with all previously recorded transactions, making something of a financial history of every movement that ever took place in the Bitcoin network.

This process is both the same and the opposite to what regular banks do. On the one hand, banks also keep a history of every transaction they process. On the other hand, unlike Bitcoin, they don't make that history available to the public. They keep it to themselves, making bank statements a much more limited resource. Now, this is supposedly done to protect the privacy of their users, but it also makes for an overall less reliable system. That is, at least, the claim that most hardcore Bitcoin advocates make.

Whether your interest in crypto is strictly as an investor or whether you share the political tone as well, the fact is no centralized financial system offers the same transparency as Bitcoin. In a regular bank, you just do your thing and hope everything is running well on the backend. It's a liberating thought because it relieves you from having to check whether everything is in order, but the price you pay is losing your autonomy. You don't know who did what, but the bank does, and they certainly use that information to build up a customer profile of you. Over time, this can make it more or less likely for you to get a home loan or other things like that. So yes, this detail can certainly have a negative effect on your plans.

The alternative, then, is decentralized finance, or DeFi for short. Mind you, not all cryptocurrencies have the same properties. For example, Bitcoin has a public blockchain that everyone can see, but privacy coins, quite understandably, don't disclose that kind of information. However, no matter what cryptocurrency you're using, you can rest assured that no secretive institution is checking out your information behind your back. And that comes at a price too. You see, in a regular bank, you lose your debit card and you can go get a new one, no sweat. With DeFi, you're in charge of everything and that means you can't lose your account information. If you do, no one will be able to help you. It's almost like being tangled up in the pile of passwords we all use nowadays, but worse.

15

There are some famous examples of this. Recently, Stefan Thomas, a cryptocurrency expert, has reportedly lost access to his 7,002 Bitcoin that he saved from payments in his job at Ripple (Carmichael, 2021), which by the way is an altcoin. He has the passcode to his crypto wallet stored in an encrypted flash drive, also known as IronKey. The problem is he can't remember the passcode to his IronKey, and he only has 10 attempts before the thing shuts close, of which he's already wasted 8. He naturally stopped trying to access the IronKey and is now looking at a Bitcoin fortune worth around 420 million dollars, although he's locked himself out of actually using it.

Similarly, one James Howells had 7,500 Bitcoin stored in a hard drive wallet back in 2013 (Browne, 2021). At the time he didn't know the cryptocurrency would become so valuable and eventually he threw away the hard drive, forgetting he had his crypto stored in it. Since then, he has made several attempts at recuperating the hard drive, but it is now lost in the middle of a trash dump.

Both examples are to show you how everything can have a good side and a bad side. In this case, we like very much the idea of a decentralized financial network that will not be constantly tracking our every move. However, like any good Spiderman movie would say, with great power comes great responsibility. Once you get your first crypto wallet and start holding crypto yourself, you need to make sure you have copies of your password in more than one place. You can trust your own good memory, but the wisest thing to do is to always have a backup, or two, or three...

## HOW IT WORKS AND WHO KEEPS IT ALIVE

The nitty gritty part of Bitcoin, and all of crypto, is the cryptography built around it. It's an integral part, but it is what gets most of us slightly put-off, at least in the beginning. Put simply, it is a system consisting of two keys, one public and one private, that every user has and uses when they are going to make a transaction. They are the equivalent of the account number you would get when opening a regular bank account.

- Sending and Receiving Crypto

Let's say you have a friend called Ben who lives in Nicaragua and has asked you to send him some crypto because it's cheaper than a bank transfer. You would then need to ask him for his public key and get to your crypto wallet to make the transaction. Most of these wallets, when creating a new account, will ask you to type a password so that you don't have to remember your actual private key, which is a long string of numbers. In any case, we will discuss the details of crypto wallets more broadly in Chapter Five.

Once you've typed in your password and you've accessed your wallet, you will find an option somewhere to type the amount you want to send and the address of the person who will receive it. Since Bitcoin is anonymous, both creating the wallet, sending or receiving crypto does not require any personal information. You type the address of the receiver, click send and then your transaction will start a process.

This is one of the areas where Bitcoin and even some altcoins have been criticized. Any regular payment processor like Visa will handle your transaction within less than a minute, but the same is not true about crypto transactions. They don't all take the same amount of time, some are more tardy than others, but they're all slower than normal transactions. The reason is they have a slightly more cumbersome process to go through.

- What goes on behind the scenes

Everything you did from your wallet has the following implications on the backend. First, you specified the details of the transaction: how much you're going to send. That part constitutes the "message." Now, the next part is where the magic happens. You take out your private key, you put it next to the message and then these two ingredients are combined. Your "signature" (meaning your authorization) is actually a combination of your message to Ben plus your private key. That means your digital signature is way better than everyday signatures, because it changes with every new transaction that you make.

Your signed message then goes to a previous midway stop called the "meme pool" (which is just short for memory pool). In this place, your message awaits confirmation. Those who have downloaded and run the Bitcoin software on their computer, known as miners, go to the meme pool and pick up a bunch of newly created messages just like your own. All these messages are legitimate, but they have yet to be validated, which will only occur once they are added to a new block by a miner. This block is then added to the end of the blockchain and that's it. It is now part of the history of transactions in Bitcoin's open ledger.

The reason this takes so long is your signed message is very well encrypted. Therefore the miners, which are just computers, some stronger than others, have to churn out for a certain amount of time before they can crack the "puzzle" and verify your transaction. They must do this for every single transaction they add to their new block, so of course it takes them a while. Also, it forces them to spend a significant amount of electricity, which is the very reason crypto networks are so harshly criticized on account of their cost in terms of electricity.

The thing is not all blocks are the same size. In the case of Bitcoin, the most popular one, blocks can only house up to seven transactions, because they have a size limit of one megabyte. Many people have argued they should just increase this limit and help make the whole transaction validation process less inefficient. I for one think that is a great idea. Anyway, I'm not so sure we can count on that happening anytime soon.

Every transaction on the planet has to go through this same procedure. Even though there are thousands of miners for pretty much every popular cryptocurrency out there, it always takes around ten minutes for a new block to be added to the blockchain. This is because the Bitcoin software sets a degree of difficulty to the cryptographic puzzle based on the computing power that existing miners amount to. In other words, the difficulty of the puzzle, which is called a hash algorithm, is variable and is adjusted to always have more or less the same difficulty.

## CRYPTO WALLETS

This is an important part for us. All the previous information about blockchain, in all honesty, is important, but not vital. If you really dig deep into the subject, you simply can't dispense with it, of course. That being said, I've seen people get around without it and not have any trouble at all, provided their purpose is investing and not mining. So that's my take on the technical bits of crypto: they're very important, but there's a bunch of things you can do as an investor without having to need them. On the other hand, one thing any good crypto investor must have absolute control over are their crypto wallets. And I say wallets in plural because you're going to need more than one.

There are three types of crypto wallets, each different from the rest because of how much security they can give you: custodial wallets, hot wallets and cold wallets. We will cover them later in the book, but suffice it to say for now that they are all basically software through which you can access, manage and exchange crypto. In other words, they aren't wallets in the traditional sense of the word. Also, there is no single right tool when it comes to choosing a crypto wallet. Some are less safe than others, but they all serve a specific purpose and you're supposed to use them all in combination. But as I said, we will cover all of this more in depth a little later.

# THE BASICS OF CRYPTO MINING

We have discussed some of this already, but not nearly enough if your interest is becoming a miner yourself. In the world of crypto, you can either be a regular user or a miner. In the former case, you just worry about getting a broad understanding of the basics, you make sure of being very careful managing your wallets and you're done. In the latter case, however, you get a bunch of additional benefits, albeit at the cost of facing a lot more technical difficulty than regular users.

Over the years, the hardware involved in crypto mining, starting with Bitcoin and beyond, has evolved according to how competitive it became. Back when Satoshi launched the first version of Bitcoin, all mining was still so simple, the total volume of transactions still so small, that mining required nothing more than a personal CPU. Any domestic computer could do the job. All you had to do was make sure it had good ventilation to be running 24/7. And the rewards were much higher too.

You see, because Bitcoin is a decentralized system, Satoshi set things up so that miners would get rewarded with newly created Bitcoin every time they successfully added a new block to the blockchain. But in order to stop the supply at 21 million, the system is also set to split the reward in half every 4 years, give or take. That means that back in 2010 the reward was ฿50, then in 2014 it went down to ฿25, then ฿12.5 in 2018, so on and so forth. The idea is that this reward is getting smaller and smaller with every day that goes by, such that in a few years mining will no longer be a profitable business model. At that point, it is said, all miners will move on to charging fees for every transaction.

- Going DIY or going all professional about it

At some point in 2010, the first GPUs were developed (Kim, 2020). Because these were designed for more specific tasks as opposed to the variety of things CPUs are in charge of, they immediately became a favorite amongst DIY miners. In fact, they're still used today, although not for Bitcoin. The thing is other cryptocurrencies, like Ether, are a little easier to mine because they're newer and also because they're not so mainstream. That makes it possible for you to set aside some three thousand dollars and be perfectly capable of putting together a mining rig with a couple GPUs, a ventilator and a motherboard. You plug that into your computer, run the necessary software for your altcoin of choice, and that's it. You just let it do its thing and every now and then you'll get rewarded for having added a new block.

As for Bitcoin, mining is much harder to do, to the point where only a company can afford the investment that is required for it. You see, once you get past GPUs, you enter a world of computers that have been specifically designed with one purpose: mining crypto. That makes them exceptionally good at their job, but also much less versatile, which means they're a very expensive piece of equipment. They go by the acronym ASIC, which means application-specific integrated circuit. A popular model such as the Antminer S19 Pro can cost you up to three thousand dollars (SoftwareTestingHelp, 2021), and you need to set up a whole farm of them if you want your mining to be competitive.

Moreover, you need to take electricity into account because crypto mining uses a lot of it. Most professional miners use solar panels to optimize their performance and they also go to great lengths to make sure their setup is electricity efficient. All of this makes Bitcoin mining a very difficult thing, and other altcoins are catching up on this really fast. At some point, it simply will not be possible to consider crypto mining a profitable business. If you're into it, make sure you hop on the wagon before that happens, and go for the lesser cryptocurrencies, which are easier and cheaper to mine.

- Publicly traded crypto mining companies

Finally, there is one last option if you really want to be involved in crypto mining, but think it is just too complicated to do it yourself. I'm referring of course to simple, straightforward investing. You can track down a number of companies that are in the crypto mining business, a lot of which are publicly traded now. You rank them out as you would with any other regular company, and when you make up your mind you can buy their stock.

Some popular examples of this sort of companies are BIT Digital, Stronghold Digital Mining and Canaan (Anthony, 2021), but there are many others. Some of them are listed in big, reputable stock exchanges, like Nasdaq or the New York Stock Exchange, so they're legit. You just need to do the same background research you would do for any other investment, and I guarantee you will find a good investment. Of course you won't be collecting rewards like miners do; your exposure to the business will be mediated. Still, it can be fun and it's actually a good way of getting closer to the crypto world without yet having to take any real steps yourself.

## THE LIGHTNING NETWORK

The problem of scalability, which is discussed further in Chapter Eight, has to do with Bitcoin's slow payment processing. One solution proposed for this is the lightning network, which is simply a second layer on top of the blockchain to process the smaller transactions (Hay, 2021). It only works for recurring transactions you do with known recipients or payers. Basically, you and your partner open up a so-called off-chain channel to record small transactions for a specific time period, say a month or a year.

This is quite similar to opening up a tab at a restaurant. Both you and the owner of the restaurant know and trust each other, so you decide to make payments more practical. You put a deposit in advance covering the cost of all the meals you'll have throughout the year, and then for the rest of this period no other payments are needed. At the end of the year, the tab can be finally recorded as a transaction, thus adding one single record for all these smaller, recurring payments you did.

The lightning network follows the same principle. It avoids having to clutter the blockchain with all sorts of small and trivial transactions by adding them up and recording them only once after a specific time period. There is no need to worry about this solution being less secure than the main blockchain because the tab, as it were, can only be opened, written on and closed with both parties' key. If one of the parties doesn't agree to put it, there can be no changes to the tab.

# CHAPTER SUMMARY

- The network on which Bitcoin and all other cryptocurrencies work is called the blockchain. It is effectively a chain of blocks, each containing a small set of transactions.
- Inside the blockchain, crypto's transaction history is stored. Unlike banks, in the case of crypto this history is made public.
- In the case of mined crypto, those in charge of issuing new coins are called miners. They all store the blockchain, so data isn't stored in one single place, but rather in many computers at the same time.
- Crypto is stored in electronic wallets and there are three types, custodial, hot and cold wallets.
- Crypto mining is done with a computer running the Bitcoin software 24/7 and validating transactions. Over time, it has become more competitive, so people use application specific computers for the task.
- Mining crypto is cost intensive in terms of electricity and gear. Before you think about doing it, be thorough about budgeting and see whether it can be profitable to you.
- Another way of profiting from crypto mining is investing in a company that does this professionally.
- The lightning network is a system to make payment processing more efficient by bundling up several small transactions into a single one.

# CHAPTER 3
# CRYPTO VS. REGULAR MONEY

A common beginner's mistake is thinking crypto is like regular money just like that. I mean, there is a vague notion that we need to internalize a rather hefty amount of know-how, but other than that we assume everything else is going to work just like we know money is supposed to work.

This is a big mistake. At least up till now, there is probably nothing that has worked less like money as cryptocurrencies have. For one thing, people primarily use them as an investment, which is not the purpose money is supposed to serve. Moreover, crypto changes in price almost as regularly as people breathe, and one of the fundamental requirements of proper money is that its value is stable. It's supposed to be a reliable haven for capital as people move about from one investment to another. You can think of it as a train station where people can shift directions and go to places. Nobody goes there wishing to stay for too long because their ultimate destination is somewhere else, but they need that in-between point and they need it to be reliable. But if money changes price too quickly, all reliability becomes impossible.

Crypto is designed to work as money, it is very well equipped to do so, but that hasn't happened yet. No matter what brought you to this book, what your plans are, that fact has to be present in your head at all times. Sooner or later, this will change and crypto will start being more broadly used the way it was intended to. But before that happens, it's important not to get confused. You certainly can and will use crypto to pay for things here and there, but not enough that you can call it a currency. You know why? It's because cryptocurrencies aren't allowed to be legal tender.

## WHAT DOES LEGAL TENDER MEAN?

Legal tender is everything that is legally authorized to settle financial transactions (Investopedia, 2021). In other words, that which has official permission from the government to be used to pay and get paid for things. Because this is a job that can only be performed by an authorized object, legal tender is universally restricted to national boundaries. It is what we all know as national currencies, like the US Dollar, the Renminbi or the Mexican Peso. Thus, for example, the US has its own national currency, China, Canada and Egypt have their own national currencies, and only in exceptional cases do we find an extra national currency, such as the Euro.

In the old days, this process used to be even more ceremonious. Money still relied on a physical token to be used, stored and circulated, so there were certain specific people who were responsible for actually issuing these physical tokens. They, like the national currency itself, required to be officially authorized for their job to ensure that no one could falsify money. They were known as masters of the mint and they worked with precious metals like bronze, gold or silver for the coinage of new money.

This is a common practice even to this day, although the way it is used has changed a lot. People are still buying coins officially minted by certain countries, there is for example the Canadian Maple Leaf, the US American Eagle and the best of them all, the South African Krugerrand. These have come a long way from what people used in older times. They are state of the art products that offer beauty as well as high tech security. However, people usually buy them as a means to store value away from money, so they're actually an alternative to national currencies. Arguably, they're also a prior step to having bullion stored in a vault.

National currencies have gradually moved away from precious metals, first to note banks that slowly turned into modern bills, but eventually they evolved even further. Most modern money, aside from a small percentage that is still in bills, exists as just a digital entry on a balance sheet. People use credit or debit cards, online transactions and QR codes for pretty much anything they do with money, so there is no longer a pressing need for it to have a physical face.

But the underlying system remains largely the same. Central banks are, by law, the only ones authorized to issue new money, making them the modern equivalent of the ancient masters of the mint. At the same time, by moving interest rates up or down, central banks can influence the eagerness of private banks to issue new credit (Dean and Pringle, 1995). These are the two forms in which money can be created in the present: either directly by the central bank or by private banks issuing credit. In both cases, all central or private banks do is add a new entry at the end of their balance sheets, so money is effectively 100% digital.

You might be wondering why, if money is all or mostly digital nowadays, cryptocurrencies are any different from it. This is a very good question because it leads to some of the biggest differences Bitcoin introduced to regular money. You see, the fact that central banks have a direct way (by issuing new money) and an indirect way (by moving interest rates) to create money means they have a monopoly over the supply of a national currency. This is no mistake, it comes by design. Central banks are ideally independent from national governments, so they can dedicate their full energy to monetary policy irrespective of political developments.

But this is of course not always true. Even in developed economies where one would expect central banks to be away from the hand of the government, it is often pointed out that certain influence between the two does take place. Above everything else, people think central banks are responsible for high inflation rates, and that money should be detached from their control altogether. That's probably the biggest difference Bitcoin introduced. Both for better and worse, the fact that it is decentralized means there is no central bank is in charge of regulating it. There is simply no one to blame for its ups and downs in price, aside from trends in speculation, of course.

## ARE CRYPTOCURRENCIES LEGAL TENDER?

No, they're not. Since they are not centralized, they also don't have permission from any government to be used to settle financial transactions. If cryptocurrencies are being used this way regardless, that is because people either believe in their benefits, they use their price shifts to make a profit, or use them as a hedge against inflation. Those are the three most popular ways in which cryptocurrencies are being used in the present, but none of them involves the participation, let alone the authorization from a government institution. In other words, cryptocurrencies aren't illegal to have, trade with or mine, but they're not legal to be used as money.

That being said, some countries are more crypto friendly than others. Now, there is an important distinction to make here, and we will discuss it further in the following chapter. Certain countries have taken serious steps towards creating their own official cryptocurrencies. These cases do not concern us in this section, because they just constitute a form of centralized cryptocurrency. It means governments are trying to catch up with the revolution started by Bitcoin, but not that they embrace it fully. Rather, they are trying to compete against it.

On the other hand, certain governments provide benefits for decentralized crypto, making it not just legal, but convenient to use.

28

Those are the ones we can consider crypto friendly and a brief list of examples would have to include Germany, Vietnam, Thailand, Singapore, Malaysia or Switzerland (Henn, 2021). In general, they give certain tax exemptions on crypto holdings, ranging from partial to full exemptions. We should perhaps include El Salvador as well because in mid 2021 the president of this country announced he would allow Bitcoin as legal tender (Renteira and Wilson, 2021). This, however, is not as groundbreaking news as Thailand's recent announcement that it will ease the use of cryptocurrencies to boost their tourism industry (Helms, 2021).

It is still uncertain whether Bitcoin and crypto in general will soon have a solid legal ground on which to stand vis-a-vis government regulations. Every crypto exchange in existence has some regulations to track the identity of users under a policy known as Know Your Client (KYC). Even then, there are a lot of things that need to change before decentralized cryptocurrencies can work as money more broadly. To this day, people still tend to shift back to regular currencies after they've finished their business with crypto.

Now, how does this affect you? We know Bitcoin, and crypto as a whole, are innovative new ways of money, but they don't work that way completely because they aren't legal tender, which means they're also unregulated. We know there are thousands of cryptocurrencies, but unlike national currencies, none of them is attached to a specific country. Moreover, we know regular money is created by central banks and that this has an influence on the rate of inflation, whereas cryptocurrencies aren't regulated by any authority. So, here's the thing. Virtually all of the risks crypto users face come from these very qualities, which is kind of tricky because all the benefits derive from them too. In other words, if you want the freedom you must accept the risks at the same time.

In Chapter Six, we will cover all the different details about what you must do to be a responsible crypto investor. For now, though, I can tell you crypto is really not that much more dangerous than money. Of course you can end up losing money with it, but this mostly happens when people aren't careful, and this isn't exclusive to crypto. Let's face it, people can be careless with basically anything. With that kind of approach, neither crypto nor regular money are going to provide you with the protection you need. There is no such thing as a full proof alternative, so although crypto is more or less the equivalent of venturing into uncharted waters, you need not take this as more than what it is: an opportunity to learn and earn a profit as you do it.

## CRYPTO AND BITCOIN IN THE CONTEXT OF REGULAR MONEY

Because they are but also aren't money, cryptocurrencies have come to be used mostly as an investment asset. Now, as I mentioned earlier, this type of usage can come in one of three ways:

- Advocacy

In this case, we find all the people who have taken a deep, critical look at crypto, who understand their risks and benefits, and have decided to invest themselves in it because they think it will prosper. I personally feel very excited about the future of crypto, but I also think it is best to leave it to you to decide whether crypto is just an investment or also an ideal for you. At any rate, one of the oldest and most simple ways people can invest in crypto is precisely advocacy.

This is how it works. Let's say you heard about Bitcoin back in 2010 and got really curious about it. You naturally investigated further and collected every headline you found on the subject, so when you heard it was possible to buy the thing, you immediately did it. Let's suppose you bought a modest sum, around 100 Bitcoin back in 2011, back when it was trading at around $0.40. As you know, Bitcoin has since then undergone a mind-blowing increase, but think about it: is there any way you could have known that would happen back in 2011? Sure, you could have felt excited and even positive that it would become widely used, but I doubt anyone could have ballparked the price Bitcoin was going to have in 2021.

Anyway, the thing is Bitcoin has risen in value. Today, those 100 Bitcoin you bought in 2011 would be worth a little less than six million dollars. And the thing is you wouldn't have been required to do any work at all to profit from that rise in value. All you would have needed to do is buy the 100 Bitcoin, put them in a safe place and forget about them for a whole decade. I reckon this is a lot of time, but so are the timeframes for any realistic retirement plan with annuities or long-term treasury bonds. The only difference is there is no way you could have saved over five million in a decade, much less with a single investment of $40!

The only potential downside is not everyone is capable of withholding their impulses and leaving their investment alone. What do you think you would have done, for instance, back in 2019 when the price of Bitcoin fell to only $3,000 after having reached $17,000 the year before? What would you do now that the price of Bitcoin fell to $57,000 after having reached more than $60,000 just a few months ago? In hindsight, anyone can go ahead and say they knew things would pick up in due time, but in reality only true hardcore Bitcoin advocates would have withstood moments of doubt.

- Short-term price shifts

The option we just saw has no other risk than that of the initial bet. Now that Bitcoin is well-known for its rocket-like price behavior, however, things are different. People still look to make a profit out of it, but not merely by awaiting big price shifts. Instead, they try to look at the price behavior itself and make many small profits by trading at a discount.

Let's say you're looking right now at a typical candlestick chart. Are you familiar with them? They are used in crypto exchanges to show not just ups and downs, but also demand. Inside the chart, every candlestick has a thick body and an upper and lower shadow.

The body represents the price at the beginning and end of a trading day, with the color being either red or green to show whether the price increased or decreased. The upper and lower shadows represent the highest and lowest prices reached within the same trading day.

So, suppose you're looking at the chart and are already somewhat familiar with it. Moreover, you know there are cycles, so when the price has been going down consistently for a period of time, it is to be expected that it should go up again, and vice versa. This is important to know so you don't panic when the curve is only just starting to go down. At that point, it is fairly possible that the price will continue to go down in the next days as well. But what should you do? If you panic and sell your crypto as the price is going down, all you can hope to do is crystalize your losses at some point in the drawdown. Now, that makes perfect sense from the point of view of emotions, but it makes no sense at all if you're following a bigger plan.

Let's enlarge our scope a bit and see how that same curve that caused you to panic looks a few days after the drawdown. It will likely start going upwards again and the price will recuperate a part, if not all, of its previous level. In some cases, it might even shoot up hard enough that the price reached a new high it didn't have before. But if you sold your crypto during the drawdown, you wouldn't have benefited from any of that. So panic is not the same as prudence. Prudence tells us what doesn't sound like a good plan, whereas panic can only play against us, making our bigger plan less clear.

The most popular type of crypto investment around price shifts is short term, which is not exactly what I described. In the short term, it becomes harder to predict whether a curve will continue to go up or down, when it will change directions and how high or how low it will go. This makes short term investment much riskier than moving along big movements in the candlestick chart. You can make quick profits and collect quite a lot of money every week, but the amount of work is more intensive and you need to know what you're doing to avoid bad outcomes.

There are two ways of short term crypto investing, one direct and the other indirect. Direct investing means you purchase a cryptocurrency and do your trading based on short term predictions about the behavior you think the price will have. Indirect investment, on the other hand, is more akin to derivatives. If you don't know what derivatives are, this is how they work. You don't buy the asset itself, but rather a contract that depends on an asset. So, for example, when you hold a future on Binance, a crypto exchange, your contract stipulates that provided the price of a cryptocurrency reaches a specific point or margin as you predicted, you will get rewarded by Binance.

Summing up, short term crypto investing can be done by trading crypto yourself or buying futures on an exchange. Both cases require scouting the price of a cryptocurrency across several exchanges. Where they differ is that trading crypto directly provides a profit from buying it at a discount and selling it again at a premium, whereas with futures your profit is a reward you get from the exchange. In the latter case, you don't sell your crypto, but rather put it as a bet footer and risk losing it if your prediction was wrong. Both are pretty risky and you should only try them after getting to know crypto in depth.

- A hedge against inflation

This form of crypto investment is the most connected to crypto's fundamental difference with regular money. As I said, all examples of regular currency are inflationary and the rate of inflation they have isn't in people's hands. Therefore all investors, be it crypto or regular investors, know they need some way to have their capital hedged against the inflationary trend of money.

Some investors buy gold and other precious metals, others buy treasury bonds or real estate, but lately even mainstream investors have shown interest in crypto as another potential hedge against inflation. The reason is simple. When you buy precious metals in bulk, you need to cover storage costs and you're not totally hedged against inflation. Since 1971, gold and other precious metals are no longer linked to the US dollar and this has led to a lot of speculation around them. So unlike what some people say, gold isn't all that stable in price.

On the other hand, treasury bonds are widely said to be "risk-free" investments, but if you're going to trust them you might as well trust regular currency, since they both come from the same source: the government. Don't get me wrong, I think treasury bills *can* be a serious investment to consider, but keep in mind they are only as solid as the government that offers them. US so-called T-bills are pretty reliable, but South American government bonds, say, aren't equally reliable.

Finally, real estate has always been a great investment since ancient times. In fact, it is probably one of the first investments that existed. There is hardly a way in which you can lose money buying property; at the very least you will keep the value of your investment. But real estate is expensive, so it is also at a different scale as investments go, whereas with crypto you can start with as little money as you want, slowly increasing the amount as you go along.

So we're left with crypto. Now, keep in mind you're not really going for the one that has the highest price outright. Your goal is to actually identify which cryptocurrencies will either stay put or undergo a significant rise in terms of price. In both cases, the behavior of the cryptocurrency has to be good enough to outperform that of the currency you're trying to hedge against. So, for example, a stablecoin would be no good. Stablecoins are cryptocurrencies that aren't mined, but rather track the price of an underlying asset, typically a regular currency. USD Coin is an example of this, and insofar as it tracks the price of the US dollar, it is stable, but constitutes no hedge against inflation.

The only way a cryptocurrency can be a hedge against inflation is if its supply is capped at a certain predetermined limit, like in the case of Bitcoin. This means Bitcoin's function of value can be known beforehand, which gives you a degree of certainty only gold could previously provide. In other words, Bitcoin's value might very well be going up and down right now, but no matter what happens it will always be capped at 21 million, and that will bring its price back to a stable level. That's the fundamental property you should be looking for in a hedge against inflation, and it's the reason many crypto investors and even mainstream investors have started to give it a serious place in their portfolio.

# CHAPTER SUMMARY

- Although crypto is designed and well equipped to work as money, it isn't used in that way.
- For something to be officially used as money, it has to be acknowledged by governments as legal tender.
- Over time, legal tender used to be bullion, then paper bank notes and now mere digital entries on the central bank's balance sheet.
- Crypto has been slowly accepted into the financial system with regulation, but it isn't accepted legally as money, so it isn't legal tender.
- In view of its amazing price increase, Bitcoin tends to be used either for advocacy, for short-selling on short-term price shifts and also to hedge against inflation.
- All of these use cases mean that Bitcoin, and by extension crypto, are being used as investment assets more than anything else.

# CHAPTER 4
## CRYPTO REGULATED?

The first cryptocurrency, Bitcoin, came to this world as an independent creation. Therefore it started out being totally free of government regulations, but this of course didn't stay like that for too long. Even though cryptocurrencies aren't legal tender, with the exception of El Salvador, there are by now a number of laws and regulations you need to know in order to sail comfortably in the crypto world.

At a global level, there are countries that have technically banned crypto, but in practice there is likely any country with no percentage of its population holding some crypto. Some countries that currently have crypto banned are, for example China, Makistan, Algeria, Ecuador or Bolivia. At the other end of the spectrum, countries that not only allow, but actively encourage the use of crypto are, for example, Canada, Japan, Australia, France, the UK or the US. The latter are countries where most crypto exchanges operate, although their services extend worldwide, at least in most cases. So, overall it can be said that in little more than a decade crypto has reached a degree of acceptance and use that is significant and will continue to grow.

However, the panorama in terms of regulations hasn't yet caught up with the growing trend of Bitcoin and other cryptocurrencies. This is due in part to plans that governments have on their own, which we will discuss in a while, but also to the fact that regulators are still uncertain about which direction to take. In short, crypto is seen in these following ways:

- An amazing innovation
- The first form of borderless money that isn't linked to any nation-state
- A potential use for money laundering and crime funding

As I'm sure you can imagine, most governments tend to gravitate towards the last entry on this list. They claim to see the benefit of crypto, but are mostly concerned with it helping the misuse of money, so naturally most proposed regulations address that very concern.

## ARE BITCOIN AND OTHER CRYPTOCURRENCIES REGULATED?

As of the present, the US, for example, has advanced proposals for regulations on crypto mostly on the basis of the Banks Secrecy Act of 1970 (Green, 2021). In other words, restrictions are proposed along the lines of setting limits on the size of transactions that can be done without providing additional personal information. These regulations are managed by the Financial Crimes Enforcement Network (FinCen), an institution that requires transactions over $3,000 and $10,000 to add information on all parties involved. Transactions over $3,000, if involving in countries that are considered problematic, must report information of the payer and the payee to FinCen. Transactions over $10,000 must do the same regardless of the countries involved.

Besides this, there are other more favorable regulations around the world. The US but also European Union, for example, accept the use of cryptocurrency for transactions, although they don't recognize it as legal tender. Within the EU, each country is free to set up their own regulations, and these mostly have to do with special tax treatments. These types of friendly regulations have been mostly advanced by nation-states to encourage an increase in their tourism revenue, since the pandemic has severely affected them. I previously mentioned the case of Thailand, for example, which seeks to recuperate the tourism revenue it lost in 2020, among other things by projecting a more solid basis for the comfort of crypto users.

There are still many areas to cover in terms of regulations, especially in the field of user protection. In the past, there have been various cases of crypto exchanges that got hacked and were unable to give any form of compensation to the users who lost their crypto in the process. This is what happened with Coincheck's 2018 hack (over $500m lost), Poly Network's 2021 hack ($600m lost), Mt Gox's hack in 2014 (over $400m lost) or KuCoin's hack in 2020 (almost $300m lost) (Bolly Inside, 2021). Because crypto exchanges provide their customers with hosted wallets that are stored in their servers, if the exchange gets hacked, customers too get hacked.

The thing is, however, that inflation in the US has steadily been rising for the past two years, so the demand for cryptocurrency has only increased. Bitcoin and Ethereum, the two most popular examples, are probably more widely accepted now than at any point in the past, and the trend is almost certainly going to continue. This in turn is bringing crypto much more to the attention of financial supervising authorities, which will likely bring along even more regulations in the near future.

So once again, what does this mean to you? It basically means two things. On the one hand, you should keep an eye on crypto prices because demand always brings prices up. On the other hand, it means more personal information will probably be required in crypto exchanges and brokers as time goes on. That affects our privacy, but it will probably offer more user protection too. In other words, it's a tradeoff.

# WHAT MOTIVATED THE CREATION OF BITCOIN

The above discussion brings us right into the main reason why Bitcoin was created in the first place. As I said in the first chapter, Bitcoin's date of creation coincides with the 2008 financial crisis. The very first block in Bitcoin's blockchain includes a quote from a headline alluding quite directly to this crisis. So clearly there is a connection between these two things. At the bottom of Bitcoin, there is not just a cool new idea about how money should work; above all, there is an attempt at saying: hey, this is not working the ways it's supposed to work, so here's what we should do.

Now, what are the pillars of that proposal? As it can be seen from Satoshi's original idea, they are basically these:

- Issuing new money is what drives inflation up, so the supply of money should be limited.
- Not only that, the supply of money should be in nobody's hands. Instead, it should be driven by a cold, perfectly impartial algorithm.
- All transactions shouldn't be kept in private by either central or private banks, but rather public and available to everyone for free.
- Money shouldn't be restrained by nationality, it should be borderless and belong to no country in particular.
- A person's bank account should be under no jurisdiction other than their own, with all passwords in their hands alone.
- Financial information should not be kept in a single central server, but rather in many smaller nodes at once, thereby allowing for more resilience in the network as a whole.
- Banking itself should be dispensed with and replaced with a peer-to-peer payment system.

One of the most obvious benefits crypto has brought with it is the inclusion of many new people to the financial system. As of 2021, it is estimated that some 1.7 billion people still have no bank account (The Economist, 2021). That is a lot of people who are still living strictly within the world of physical cash, which means they don't benefit from any of the comforts technology has brought to finance, even before the arrival of Bitcoin.

Another big contribution of Bitcoin and other cryptocurrencies is that they make international transactions cheaper and faster. Suppose, for example, that you need to send money from Europe to Central America. To make things a little more realistic, suppose you are an immigrant interested in sending a remittance to your relatives back in Honduras. This is a very typical case in which people not only want to send money; they absolutely need that it be cheap and quick. Crypto provides them with both things and, at least outside the context of crypto investment, it does not require them to introduce any personal information.

Things like this have definitely shown people all around the world that the potential of cryptocurrencies is huge. Be it as an investor, a trader, a broker or a mere generic user, it helps bring money closer to you than ever before. Things are easier to control; national barriers are easier to go through and security is state of the art. Yes, I know we discussed some hacking assaults in the past, but this is due to crypto's decentralized nature, not to basic security flaws in its design. The overall idea is just positive in so many regards that it is hard to understand why crypto didn't get more acceptance from governments. In other words, why it hasn't yet been used as regular money by a majority of the population.

So what prevented this from happening? In a nutshell, it was the very lack of regulation that Bitcoin demanded, which other cryptocurrencies followed completely. In the absence of a regulatory body, Bitcoin became subject to wild and widespread speculation. For evidence of this, look no further than its price fluctuations. Bitcoin and other cryptocurrencies have had price shifts of well over 20% as a matter of everyday life. In the world of real currencies, that is simply unthinkable. So a lot of people have benefited from an overall uphill trend that, as I said, brought Bitcoin's price truly to the skies. People who were lucky enough to buy it when it was almost free, have found themselves rich out of nowhere.

Now, this is all nice and fascinating. It is, in fact, the very reason we're here: to make money out of crypto investing. However, it must be said that the reason we're interested in crypto as a potential investment is the very reason it can't yet work as proper money. Money is supposed to guarantee it will be the same now and later in time. That's what you would call a store of value. But Bitcoin is unable to work as a store of value because its price varies so wildly that you can't be sure your money will be the same tomorrow. It might go up, sure, but even in that case it couldn't be said that it kept its value.

It is fair to say, then, that although Bitcoin was created around a critique to the financial system, this is still evolving as time goes by. There are still many unknowns about it and we shall only see where all of this leads at a later date in the future.

## THE QUESTION OF CBDCS

The biggest challenge to the future of decentralized crypto, lately, has come from the very institutions Bitcoin intended to criticize: central banks. The acronym you see up there, CBDCs, stands for Central Bank Digital Currencies. Reportedly in an attempt at appreciating the necessary innovations that Bitcoin put on the table, central banks have expressed their interest in creating cryptocurrencies of their own. I'm sure you can imagine these wouldn't be decentralized, so of course the idea is just a partial adoption of Bitcoin's original design. In other words, central banks like the techy side of Bitcoin's innovations, but they don't like the idea of losing control over the supply and supervision of national currencies.

CBDCs have been debated in one way or another for a number of years now, in fact even before the creation of Bitcoin. However, it wasn't until 2020 that a large number of the world's most prominent central banks, around 86%, started taking serious steps in that direction (Boar and Wehrli, 2021). This means they are researching the subject before taking any definitive measures, so it is still uncertain what they will do in the end. Mind you, changes are very likely to arrive sooner that you would think. For example, China has announced its plans to launch a digital version of their currency on the occasion of the 2022 Olympics, which will be hosted in Beijing.

One of the trends that indicates doing this would be wise on the part of central banks is the recent rise in demand for stablecoins. As I said in Chapter One, stablecoins are cryptocurrencies that are pegged to the value of some underlying asset, typically a regular currency. USD Coin, for example, is set to be always at a one to one ratio with the value of the US dollar. Now, once you're trading with crypto, it is logical to assume that switching back and forth with real currencies is more costly than staying within the crypto "ecosystem," if you will. Therefore you can exchange your Bitcoin for USD Coin and get a much better deal than if you exchanged it for regular dollars. People are aware of this advantage, so they've been using it more and more, which resulted in a trend that suggests an overall preference for stablecoins over regular currency.

Another similar indicator is found in the market capitalization of some of the biggest cryptocurrencies in existence. As of November 2021, these were the highest recorded market caps (Yahoo Finance, 2021):

- Bitcoin (BTC): $1.07 trillion
- Ethereum (ETH): $554.14 billion
- Binance Coin (BNB): $105.02 billion
- Tether (USDT), a stablecoin pegged to the US dollar: $73.62 billion

In view of these factors, central banks believe they not only need to create their own cryptocurrencies, they also need to do it quickly.

The more they wait while decentralized crypto grows in market cap, the harder it will be to reclaim that market share with their own alternative.

What's to be expected from this? Well, there are two consequences you need to be wary of. The most immediate one is that CBDCs would render private banks totally unnecessary. You see, given that crypto is designed to be a peer-to-peer payment system, it requires no intermediary body making transactions possible. Instead, money would be transferred directly from the central bank into your personal account. It would also be directly transferred from your bank account to that of someone else, and vice versa. In other words, all transactions would be more efficient, but in the process they would cause the role of private banks to disappear.

The second consequence of interest to you is directly related to the first one. In short, the same efficiency would open the door for total control on the side of central banks, even more than before. Imagine, for example, what would happen if a government weren't democratic and disagreed with the kinds of newspapers you're subscribed to. For them, it would be as simple as freezing your bank account, which is now linked directly to them, and restricting the use of your money to keep paying for those subscriptions. In other words, they could very easily put limits on what you can and cannot buy with their CBDCs. This is of course totally the opposite of what Bitcoin was created for, and it's a very real danger too. Decentralized crypto has shown to have many risks, but none is comparable to that of a centralized cryptocurrency under the control of an authoritarian government.

All in all, CBDCs are almost certainly going to be a reality in the not too distant future, so you must be prepared for them. They will also be both very similar and very different from today's decentralized cryptocurrencies. The risks and benefits that CBDCs pose are potentially just as radical as those we've discussed for crypto so far, so you shouldn't make the mistake of thinking they're the same thing.

# CHAPTER SUMMARY

- Some countries are more friendly to crypto than others, some have even started accepting it as a means of payment. However, it is still not legal in the full sense anywhere.
- Most crypto related regulations are based on the Bank Secrecy Act of 1970. These regulations mostly deal with imposing limits on how much you can transfer without the need for personal information.
- Several famous hacker attacks throughout crypto's history have convinced government authorities of the need for regulation. This helps reduce the risks of using crypto, but it also interferes with the freedom it can give.
- Crypto has addressed several critical areas in mainstream finance, particularly inflation.
- Given the size of the market cap of some of the most notable cryptocurrencies, central banks feel they can no longer ignore their presence. Their latest response to this are so-called CBDCs, central bank digital currencies.

# CHAPTER 5
# BITCOIN'S REAL NATURE

I mentioned most money nowadays, whether it's regular currency or crypto, has no real physical existence. Although this is true, there are still some major differences to point out between currency and cryptocurrency in these modern digital times. The starting point to do so is undeniably Bitcoin, the first cryptocurrency ever created, and to this day one of the benchmarks in terms of where crypto should go next.

As we saw at the beginning, Bitcoin originated in a way that almost seems fictional in hindsight. Within that unlikely first appearance, there were two main audiences with whom Bitcoin really resonated deeply. One of them were economic libertarians who, whether tech savvy or not, saw Bitcoin as an alternative to all the evils of the mainstream financial system. On the other side of the spectrum, there were those who knew enough about computers or cryptography to appreciate the mere jaw dropping accomplishment on its own, regardless of where it would lead in the end.

In a way, these two worlds converged and they did so around a new concept on intangible money. Around it all, as I mentioned in the beginning there was the 2008 financial crisis around subprime mortgages (Kosakowski, 2021). This crisis exploded first in the US, but quite soon spread across all corners of the world as if it were something of a different nature, like a natural disaster of some kind. The crisis took down some major players, like Lehman Brothers, and forced several others to restructure.

All of this of course caused a major surge of distrust in stock markets, the global financial system and even economics as a whole. Many became impoverished and had to see their whole lives change for the worse overnight. People started looking at banking with a more cynical view and went on to denounce both private and central banks for being the very mechanisms that had engineered the problem. People's savings, they argued, were slowly and secretly being drained out of purchasing power due to one key element that up to that point had only been discussed by those well versed in economics. I am referring, of course, to inflation. From the moment inflation became the target of criticism, it became clear to all Bitcoin advocates what crypto was about.

## CRYPTO'S ECONOMIC APPROACH

Believe it or not, there is one man whose traditional economic ideas didn't differ from those of Bitcoin's creator. The man in question is Milton Friedman, Nobel prize in economics and in many ways the guru of the Chicago liberal economic school. Very much in line with one of Bitcoin's key tenets today, Friedman too believed there should be no single human criteria in charge of defining monetary policy. In other words, he thought inflation rates should be set by a perfectly impartial equation, as opposed to the humanly fallible way in which central banks work even today.

Friedman explicitly said he believed the internet would have a huge impact on modern finance (Friedman, 2012). Moreover, he thought this influence would accomplish two key things:

- It would reduce the role of the government in monetary policy.

- It would allow for the invention of true electronic money in a way that didn't exist before.

To be clear, the way things are supposed to work, the government itself isn't the force that regulates money. It is central banks that do this job, and they are independent from the government, at least in theory, and in most modern developed economies, also in point of fact. Either way, these keys to Bitcoin's functioning have truly become a reality, as Friedman predicted. In the world of Bitcoin, money has a limited supply and it ultimately isn't regulated by anybody.

But the question of electronic money is not that easy to summarize. Now, we can't really learn enough cryptography that we will understand every single detail, but we can at least brush over some key features. We discussed some of it back in Chapter Two, but now let us get a deeper idea of how crypto actually works.

In cryptography, there are a number of algorithms that can shield information and make sure it doesn't get tampered with from one point to another. This is actually the backbone of cryptocurrencies and sadly it's something us regular users can never hope to have more than a shallow understanding. On the other hand, when we're talking about centralized currencies, measures of security are mostly on the side of the service provider. Banks can afford to be at the very center of the financial system because they are in charge of providing these measures of security. As mere users, you and I get an account number, a passcode and that's about it. There's no more hassle of any kind and no concern as to how sound and secure things are on the backend because, well, we don't really wonder about that.

So the first commitment one must make when taking a serious interest in Bitcoin, and by extension in crypto as a whole, is grasping the cryptography on which they work. Now, this is not the same for all cryptocurrencies, but let's stick with Bitcoin as our demo example. Bitcoin works with a particular kind of algorithm known as Sha 256. This particular instrument is part of the hash family of algorithms. They are basically very long numbers that can come in different sizes, 16, 32 or any other multiple of 16, like for example 256. Their distinctive characteristic is that their last number changes even if so much as one single digit changes in the rest of the string. Therefore you get an immediate feedback even with so much as a tiny change has taken place.

In the case of Sha 256 in particular, we get a number that is, as many have said, beyond astronomical in size (Sanderson, 2021). To give ourselves a vague idea of the sheer size of this number, it would be equal to 2 to the 32, but multiplied by itself 8 times. In other words, this would roughly be equivalent to multiplying 4 billion by itself 8 times. As Sanderson explains, that's more or less a figure we can finally understand, but above all we can draw one key conclusion from it, which is that it far exceeds the computing power of a regular personal computer.

This system allows every message, or in this case every transaction, to be codified once again every single time. Your key alone doesn't make up the whole message, but rather the key and the contents of the transaction are combined each time to assemble a new 256 long string of digits. If you make a change, the whole number changes with it, and only a public key at the other end can decrypt it without resorting to guesswork. Now, this makes for highly trustworthy cryptography, but it also makes computers purr and heat up. Those computers in the blockchain that perform as miners can only guess how to decrypt each message, which is why mining is rewarded with newly created crypto in the first place. It is intended to give miners an incentive.

But what does that have to do with Bitcoin's economic approach, you may ask. Well, it has at least two implications. On the one hand, it points directly to one of the major logistic problems Bitcoin has today: its enormous electricity consumption. Computers need to burn a lot of energy in the process of doing their guesswork, and that has a high cost in electricity. On the other hand, it also points to the fact that traditional banking actually offers very little by way of user security. If we want modern money to be really secure, it will have to incorporate Bitcoin's methods one way or another, and users will have to be more responsible about not losing their keys.

To be fair, it must be said that Bitcoin's electricity costs are a direct consequence of it being a decentralized financial instrument. In other words, since it started out having nothing similar to public planning, several logistic questions about it are still being discussed and addressed only now. They were to be expected and the question now is how to solve them as opposed to just making derogatory comments on the subject. For instance, several other cryptocurrencies have attempted to solve Bitcoin's problem. They attempt to replace Bitcoin's costly decryption process, known as Proof of Work (PoW), with something less inefficient.

Ethereum, for instance, has plans to launch a new version around 2022 (McQuaid, 2021) that would switch its old PoW implementation for a brand new Proof of Stake (PoS) method. The difference between PoW and PoS, or mining and staking, fundamentally comes down to the way in which transactions are validated and new crypto is created. In PoW, miners are in charge and they all compete by pulling transactions, as I said in Chapter Two, from the meme pool. This is what many have criticized as being inefficient since it implies all outstanding computers do the same work before they're even chosen. In the case of PoS, computers aren't called miners, but just plain validators, and they are chosen randomly by the system itself. This way they don't compete and they avoid doing unnecessary work when they haven't been chosen.

Another big advantage to staking is that it allows for even more decentralization than Bitcoin. You see, over time Bitcoin has spontaneously moved on from a miners base to a series of mining pools, which are groups of miners who now exert the largest control. This is worrisome for Bitcoin's advocates because it may affect decentralization, one of Bitcoin's central tenets. If mining pools have a monopoly over the creation of new Bitcoin, they can choose to do all sorts of things that could hurt its integrity, like for instance issuing false Bitcoin.

The same is not a concern for staking because no one gets to choose who will be the next validator. The software assigns a different computer at random and, moreover, it makes sure to not assign the role too many times to any computer on its own. In other words, things are designed to spread control rather than centralizing it.

## MINING AND STAKING

If you're here with an interest in crypto investment, chances are you're not also interested in becoming a miner or validator yourself. That being said, good investment practice will require you to have a basic understanding of both these highly technical activities. Let's get a look at them one by one from an investor's standpoint.

- Mining

Especially at this point in time, it's fair to say crypto mining isn't profitable for all cases. Bitcoin mining, for instance, is highly competitive in terms of hardware requirements, as I said in Chapter Two. This is why joining a mining pool can look like an attractive alternative. In a nutshell, mining pools are groups of individual miners who join their computing power to increase their chances of validating blocks at a higher rate.

There are several things to consider when deciding whether joining a mining pool is a good idea. First off, you must look at the hash rate, meaning the speed at which a particular pool claims to solve hash algorithms, be it Bitcoin's Sha 256 or any other. Besides that, there are questions we previously discussed, like electricity consumption and the degree of difficulty involved in solving hash puzzles. These things will have a direct impact on the profitability of your plan, so it's very important you look them up before making any decision.

Then there are cost and reward related aspects as well. Mining pools charge you a fee every time a reward has been obtained, since you're benefiting from a combined effort which was coordinated by the pool managers. Always make sure you check whether this fee isn't too high so that it doesn't hurt your profits either. Also along those lines, given the price of crypto is fundamentally unpredictable, check how high is the price of the cryptocurrency you have chosen to mine. If it isn't high at some point, then all other factors considered, it might be that you can't make a profit even in ideal circumstances.

To avoid being overwhelmed by all these considerations, you can help yourself with an online mining calculator. You will find many just by typing those words on a browser, but some of the most well-known are Minerstat and Cryptocompare. These sites will simply require you to input the information I just explained to you and they'll give you a quick assessment.

Other than this, I should also warn you against so-called cloud and web mining products you may find out there. You see, before joining a mining pool, you'll still be required to assemble a mining platform of your own. This makes perfect sense because you must be a miner in order to join a mining pool. However, with cloud and web mining all you need to do is download an app or visit a website. This alternative sounds too good to be true because it is. For one thing, you generally don't get any guarantee as to which cryptocurrency they will reward you with. Moreover, mining with a cell phone or a personal computer is technically possible, but not competitive by any stretch of the imagination. You will most likely burn your battery and get the littlest of all rewards, which amounts to an unprofitable alternative. This tends to get the attention of many people because of how easy it seems, but I advise you to stay away from it and stick to realistic solutions instead.

- Staking

In this case, you first need to have a stake in something, hence the name. You must put a certain amount of your own crypto as an initial deposit and have it there as a guarantee to be randomly chosen every now and then to forge new crypto. For example, in the case we discussed earlier, Ethereum, the required stake amounts to 32 ETH, which in today's ETH valuation is equivalent to around $130,000. As you can see, it is a serious amount of money and that's because it is not a scam. It sounds difficult and costly, but it is also a realistic business opportunity.

Whereas mining rewards the specific computer or pool that solved a hash puzzle, staking spreads every reward amongst all existing validators. The size of the main reward is always the same and the slice each validator gets varies depending on how many validators there are. This implies that the number of validators is regulated; in fact, only 900 new validators are allowed to join Ethereum's network every day. There is a long list of people waiting to become validators, so if you're interested in this alternative, be sure to keep that in mind. Also take into account that staking, like mining, is technically demanding and requires you know enough about crypto in order to do it appropriately.

But there is an easier way to benefit from staking without actually doing it yourself. Exchanges offer you the possibility to stake through another validator in exchange for a fee. This type of staking service is as easy for regular users as doing any other form of regular crypto transaction. The only thing you'd need to worry about is checking that fees aren't too high. One of the benefits you get with staking services like these is you can withdraw your crypto at any time, even before the validation/reward process has reached the end. But of course, doing this goes with a small additional fee for early removal.

# CAN I PHYSICALLY HOLD AND TOUCH BITCOIN?

Now, I know all of this might sound a bit like video game stuff for the uninitiated. If you feel this way too, I want you to consider two things. First, that mining and staking are activities you and I can profit from now because we are still going through crypto's early stages. The supply method for every cryptocurrency varies, but they all have some way of creating new tokens for people to use. That's the whole reason we discuss mining and staking, because in the absence of an entity similar to a central bank, they're the way in which crypto gets created. So that's number one, and it's important you know crypto will not be issued forever. The mining and staking processes will all reach an end when the supply limit has been reached, at which point miners and validators will switch to being payment service providers, like Visa.

The second thing you must consider is all other traditional forms of payment, transaction and issuance of money are equally abstract. We may think crypto is far too unfathomable because it lacks any physical form of existence, but this is all in our heads. In reality, crypto is no more digital than regular money is nowadays. They both exist as mere entries in a balance sheet. The only differences are: 1) that crypto's balance sheet is public whereas bank's balance sheets are only accessible to themselves, and 2) that crypto mining and staking are meant so no one decides when new tokens are issued, whereas regular money is issued by a decision from bankers. We already discussed what reasons stand behind crypto's change in these two regards, so when you really think about it, crypto simply seems more complicated than it actually is.

However, it is true that you can hold and touch a one dollar bill in your hands. Some people even go out of their way to keep cash in this way in safe deposit boxes, under their mattress and whatnot. This is considered a fairly old fashioned way of using regular money, but it exists. However, with crypto this is no longer possible. You either use it and trade with it through a digital platform or you don't have it at all. Crypto is the first form of money that only exists on a digital platform. This of course causes many people to feel rather nervous, like they don't really have control over it because they have no way of actually looking at it or touching it.

Those who are familiar with digital transactions still tend to insist on having some kind of material asset, like bullion or jewels. In all honesty, this isn't a silly strategy, but we shouldn't confuse it with distrusting electronic money altogether. Crypto is just as real as any other form of printed money. In fact, as we discussed, it provides more security measures than before as well as more ease of use. In reality, there is little printed money in the world. Most things are done digitally anyway, so you shouldn't fool yourself and think electronic money isn't real. The fact that you can't touch it isn't a disadvantage. On the contrary, it is what makes crypto such a useful and practical tool.

Similar to QR codes and electronic transactions, you can use crypto through a cell phone or a computer and dispense with your wallet for good. In terms of what you can do, the sky's the limit. Sure, you must be extra careful about security because, as I said, decentralized money means you have no entity protecting you from above. But this also means you have no entity watching your every move. In other words, your freedom is your own responsibility. In the following chapter, we will discuss how to use crypto so you can take charge of that responsibility in full.

# CHAPTER SUMMARY

- Crypto's economic approach is, in a way, similar to that of modern liberal economist Milton Friedman. Like him, crypto also aims at reducing government intervention as much as possible.
- Friedman predicted the advent of an electronic form of money that would finally displace the role of governments in the economy.
- Instead of the government, crypto has supply set impartially by an algorithm, so it always runs at the same pace no matter what.
- Hash algorithms are a form of cryptography that produces global changes for minor edits in the content of a message. The hash algorithm used in Bitcoin is called SHA 256.
- Before adding a new block to the blockchain, miners need to decrypt the SHA 256 encrypted message.
- This process, known as Proof of Work, requires them to spend computing power, which is what validates the transaction and also causes Bitcoin to be so costly in terms of electricity.
- Another less wasteful method, championed by Ethereum, is called Proof of Stake.
- Both mining and staking are hard to get into, technically demanding and not always profitable.
- Crypto is an all-digital form of money, therefore it is intangible. You can only access it through electronic wallets.

# CHAPTER 6
# USER'S MANUAL

There is a slightly hefty learning curve to overcome to be able to benefit from crypto without any serious issues along the way. It doesn't just come down to the fact that you can't touch crypto; that in a way is a first time anecdote and nothing more. Beyond that, there are basic questions you need to answer in as precise a way as you possibly can. You must learn where you're supposed to buy crypto, how you can trade with it and who you can do it with. You also need to learn how you can store crypto safely and how to manage that storage in a way that doesn't lead to further risks. All of these questions are important because they're a matter of everyday use. Individually, they don't pose great challenges, but it's the regularity that can cause us to trip.

If you look up Google trends, you will see that the rate at which people look up the word Bitcoin has steadily increased since the moment it was created. This reflects how interest in crypto has developed over the past decade, but it also shows how unaware most people are about it. Although curiosity has been widespread, many people have resisted their own urge to enquire further out of intimidation. They look at Bitcoin or an altcoin and they feel there's too much to learn, too many ways to end up losing money in the end. Now, although this has changed dramatically over time, it's important to stay loyal to the spirit of prudence anyway.

There are now crypto wallets (which we will discuss later) that are very friendly to the user. In the old days it used to be the case that you had to run a piece of software on a hard drive, but even this would pose some challenges to the average user. So opening a crypto wallet nowadays is not too different from opening up a Facebook account. The downside to this is that ease can cause many people to ignore the risks of crypto, and indeed it has. People can lose their passcodes or simply believe that having an online crypto wallet is good enough. Both things, along with others that we will discuss in this chapter, are wrong. You need to remember that having crypto carries more than the average responsibility we're used to having. You're in charge of more things and you need to take precautions to avoid unpleasant surprises along the way.

## HOW TO ACQUIRE AND USE CRYPTO?

One of the things you might be wondering about is where you're supposed to get crypto. It's not like you can just go to a bank or a store and ask for it. There are specialized places for this and there is a procedure you must follow. As a matter of fact, a prior step would be that you get a crypto wallet, although in this case we'll cover that in the next section. Since you'll have nothing to store before you actually get some crypto, I decided to put this section first, but feel free to jump forward if you will. Either way, the ways of properly and safely acquiring and storing crypto are the two first things you will have to do, no matter what plans you have in mind.

There are two places to obtain crypto, one option is reaching out to another user like you or me and the other option is going to a crypto exchange. In the case of going to an exchange, you will have to go through the typical KYC policy we discussed earlier in the book. In compliance with some initial regulations that were imposed on crypto, the exchange will ask you to produce some personal information in order to register. There might be some differences depending on the exchange, but these are the areas that the regulations will cover (Chen, 2021):

- Name
- Date of birth
- Address
- Employment Status
- Identification numbers
- Income

So there is a lot of paperwork to go through before so much as entering an exchange. Moreover, the amount of tools you can use in them are already pretty complex in themselves. This is clearly something you shouldn't do on your own if you're only just starting out. In the beginning, and although fees will be a bit higher for sure, you could resort to a broker instead. Brokers are almost the same as exchanges, except for the fact that they specialize in offering a service that is friendly to the non-savvy. It isn't ideal to go to them after you've learned to go on your own, but in the beginning it's not a bad idea to pay a little extra and get qualified assistance in return.

That being said, there is an even better alternative to get crypto for the first time and on the cheap. Find someone who does have crypto and has some experience using it as well. Of course, don't just go out on social media and get in contact with the first person you find. It should be someone you know in person and whom you trust, like a friend, a relative or a colleague. If you prefer, you could do this before even looking for an exchange or a broker. That way you'll avoid having to do any complicated paperwork before you get a taste of the first basic steps.

If you end up reaching out to a trusted friend, the way you'll acquire crypto is by direct peer-to-peer transaction. In reality, the same would apply in the exchange, but in this case you'll know who you're doing business with. So, you can just pay them in dollars the same way you'd pay for a meal at a restaurant. You would be effectively purchasing crypto anyway, only in an over the counter context. Then after you get a crypto wallet and you exchange public keys with this person, you could receive crypto from them and be in possession of your first crypto purchase.

When choosing between these options, just remember you cover two key questions. The first question is: have I researched enough to know how to proceed on this? And the second is: which of these alternatives makes me feel most comfortable and secure? There is no single right answer to these questions. The only priority is to choose what suits you best.

## HOW TO STORE CRYPTO?

Either way, though, you'll only ever be able to receive crypto after you get a wallet in which to do so. For this too you have a number of options, but unlike in the previous section, here you must master all options and make use of them all.

There used to be only one kind of wallet, as I said. You'd have to download the Bitcoin software, for example, and run it yourself on a hard drive. That was supposed to be your wallet. But now there are three types of crypto wallets to choose from. Most people who lack the experience tend to go for only one of these, but as I said the wise move is to use them in combination. So let's see what each of them are about first.

- Custodial Wallets

As their name implies, these are managed by someone else and are effectively out of your control. You may be wondering why on earth someone would want their crypto to be in the hands of someone else, but it's actually very important to have this alternative. You see, all trading needs an intermediary. Be it regular money or crypto, this rule applies to both all the same. In our case, crypto exchanges are the entity that performs as intermediary. But here's the thing. In order to avoid having to perform transfers directly into your crypto wallet every single time, exchanges provide you with their own custodial crypto wallets.

On the surface, there is not much difference between these and the rest, other than your accessing them through the exchange. You have an account and a separate balance for every single cryptocurrency you hold, same as you would in any other case. Every time you buy or sell crypto, these transactions are done with your custodial wallet. The only potential problem begins with leaving your crypto in there over extended periods of time. Keep in mind that their primary purpose is practicality. After your trading has ended, say at the end of the day, there is no longer a reason for you to keep using the custodial wallet. You can just move your crypto back to your personal wallet and feel more secure that way.

But why would leaving your crypto in a custodial wallet be risky? The question may seem so silly that we dare not ask, but it really is important. Once again, the source of risk comes down to decentralization. Crypto exchanges offer no insurance and have no deeper regulation beyond the KYC policies. They are, in short, quite useful and transparent entities, but subject to many dangers, their primary enemy being cyberattacks. As you may recall, I mentioned a number of famous hacking attacks that targeted crypto exchanges in the past and all the way up to the present. Quite simply, these attacks are a reality we can't afford to ignore. It isn't that exchanges themselves are dangerous, but they concentrate high volumes of traffic, so they're naturally an ideal hacking candidate.

This is why it's important you don't use custodial wallets more than you need to. As a general rule, you should withdraw your money at the end of every trading day. Doing this will become a cumbersome chore you will feel very tempted to avoid, since there are days in which you won't do much trading at all. You might think to yourself: "what's the point of moving my crypto in and out of the exchange if it costs me a small fee and it adds more hassle?" Now, that may very well be true, but the fact is there are no ideal solutions for everything. If you want to avoid losing crypto for being careless, then you simply must move it in and out every single day. It's a hassle, but it's better than having the exchange hacked with your crypto in it.

- Hot Wallets

Besides custodial wallets, there are two types of personal wallets you can and must have. The first of them are so-called hot wallets. Once again, it's worth pointing out that the nickname itself, "hot" wallets, implies that they're still relatively risky. Hot wallets are very convenient in that you aren't required to produce any personal information to open them (not even your name) and the process itself is almost identical to that of creating a Facebook account. Now, there are premium versions of the same product, generally to allow for more variety in the cryptocurrencies you can hold. But since you're not going to use hot wallets as a standalone, you can simply go with the free version and concentrate your investments on cold wallets instead.

The source of risk in hot wallets is basically the same as with exchanges and their custodial wallets. The companies that provide the service of hot wallets concentrate a large amount of users, some of them with large amounts of crypto in their balance. It's only natural to expect these large concentrations to be another attractive target for hackers. So although you would normally withdraw your money from a custodial wallet and into a hot wallet, it's important you don't use the latter for particularly large amounts. They're very comfortable to use and they allow you to pay for things on the go, but they can still be hacked relatively easily. All large amounts of crypto should be in custodial or hot wallets only as their stopping points before the final destination.

- Cold Wallets

And the final destination is this. Again, as their name implies, cold wallets are the safest ones. The reason for this is simple: they are designed to totally disconnect from the internet whenever they're not being used. Unlike custodial and hot wallets, cold wallets are actually pieces of hardware that look almost like a hard drive. They are costly too. Buying a Trezor or Ledger cold wallet, the two most famous brands out there, will cost you at least $100 just for the device. Upon receiving them, you're supposed to plug them into your computer and run their software, get your keys and that's it. Every time you need to access your wallet, you plug it in once again, knowing that when you unplug it, it will be cold dead. No matter how talented a hacker is, they won't even be able to reach it.

Nowadays, cold wallets also offer a mobile app to access them indistinctly from different devices. They also have the largest storage, with the option to store up to thousands of different cryptocurrencies, depending on the make and model.

Because no single wallet does it all, you're supposed to use cold wallets together with the other two. In short, you do your trading with custodial wallets, you take care of everyday payments with hot wallets, and you keep large amounts safe with cold wallets. Now that you know this, don't be one of those people who think they're supposed to choose only one of these alternatives. Instead, use all three in combination.

## TIPS AND RISKS

The most common misconception we must let go of is thinking that crypto is inherently unsafe. Bitcoin is comparatively safer than most traditional fintech and certain altcoins, especially privacy coins, provide even more security than Bitcoin does. In reality, the weak spot tends to be us users. Since there is no central authority in any cryptocurrency, there is no one who can assist us beyond the occasional tip. This may cause us to fall in despair every now and then, but the solution to it is quite simple: be very careful at all times and everything should run smoothly. So here are some tips on how you can do just that.

- Your private key

Number one is not losing access to your crypto wallet or wallets. As I said several times by now, having a wallet involves managing two keys, one private and one public. These two keys aren't stored in any central database like they would in, say, a Facebook account. We all know that when we forget the password to access our Facebook account, we can simply click on the "forgot password" tab and a link to renew the password will be sent to our email or cell phone. This is doubtless very convenient, but it's only possible when a central entity is in charge of managing all operations.

The difference in crypto is that no such central entity exists. Even with stablecoins, which have a more centralized type of management, no one can get access to your private key. If you lose it, no one can help you recover it. So you really need to have a system to make sure you don't lose it. You can have it stored in more than one place at a time, you can repeat it to yourself every day to make sure you remember it by heart. Whichever solution suits you best, the idea is you don't ever treat it casually. It is arguably more important than anything else.

- Avoiding theft with custodial wallets

Since you're probably going to use the custodial wallet a lot for transactions, games and payments, you could end up leaving crypto in it for more than a day on occasion. I know I said you shouldn't, but the reality is that it will happen to you eventually, like it does to all of us at least once. To help give you peace of mind if and when this happens, you can pay extra special attention to the quality of your password for this wallet.

You can make this password especially long, put uncommon characters in it and make sure it isn't the same as that of any other account you have. This is standard advice for anything that has to do with passcodes and personal accounts, so you should actually do it everywhere else as well. But it's extra important in accounts that you know in advance are subject to a higher risk.

- Password managers

Better still, no one can think of the best passwords for every single account that they have. Instead of trying, just get a password manager. There are several excellent free options out there, like for example LastPass or Bitwarden. These solutions relieve you from the burden of having to come up and remember every single password. Just thinking about what was discussed here, you would need to have three additional passwords for all three types of crypto wallets —that's a lot to manage. Wouldn't you prefer to have one password to rule them all? Moreover, you would get top notch security measures with a password manager, like two factor authentication. That way stealing your password won't be enough to access your wallets and you'll know when someone has tried to do it behind your back.

- Which network to use

It's simple: don't ever access your wallets through a public wifi connection. Let's say, for example, that you're on your way to catch a flight, you just saw the price of Bitcoin going down and wish to switch what you have for a stablecoin. This is a reasonable impulse, but given that you're at an airport you can only connect to your wallets through wifi. In such a case, you should resist the urge and wait till you get to a trusted network. It's one thing to have your email account hacked by accident, but quite another to invite thieves to your crypto account. The latter is simply more serious than regular personal accounts and you should treat it with special care under all circumstances. If you think you absolutely must access your crypto wallets in spite of being on a public wifi network, make sure you use a VPN to do so. That will at least shield you a bit more against potential threats.

# CHAPTER SUMMARY

- You can either buy crypto from an exchange or a person you know and trust. If it's the first time, I recommend the latter.
- Exchanges require you to produce personal information and, in general, the registration process isn't quick. It takes a few days before it is completed.
- As I said in the beginning, but now in more detail, there are three ways for you to store crypto: custodial wallets, hot wallets and cold wallets.
- Custodial wallets are contained in the exchange's server. They are necessary for you to trade with, but they are also risky.
- Hot wallets are personal wallets you open for free and with no personal information required. These too are contained in the service's servers, so they aren't 100% secure.
- Cold wallets are hardware based and designed to unplug from the internet when you're not using them. They are the safest option.
- You must keep your keys in good care because no one can help you recover them. Alternatively, you can use a password manager and make things easier for yourself.
- Don't ever access your wallets on wifi unless you do it with a VPN.

# CHAPTER 7
# IS CRYPTO AN ACCOMPLISHMENT?

Quite recently, in an interview for Bloomberg, the world famous investor Ray Dalio said he believes Bitcoin is "one hell of an invention" (Schatzker, 2021). He also went on to say that it is "a remarkable accomplishment," although he believes that if it were to become "really successful," it's possible it might be "killed off" by governments.

It is hard to hear those words and not have mixed feelings about whether Dalio is looking at the cryptoverse with condescension or genuine enthusiasm. His words feel like a pat on the back, but then again they also sound like reserved curiosity from afar, not much more than that. Moreover, he does not mention other cryptocurrencies; he speaks about Bitcoin alone, which suggests he's not even going to take a look at the rest.

For us, crypto is undeniably a huge accomplishment, no matter how traditional investors feel about it. That being said, to understand and assess this more thoroughly, it's important to have a look at the outside world and see what it has to say. This is where Dalio's approach turns out to be pretty instructive. He doesn't only give us a taste of the general feeling around crypto from a traditional standpoint. Above all, he points to the direction of what traditional investment has decided to use crypto for, at least for the time being.

How have they decided to use crypto, you may ask. Well, in a way that is not so different from ours, it turns out. You see, traditional investors also despise sitting on cash because they too are aware of the deleterious effects that inflation has on it. They've been looking for alternatives to cash long before crypto came into the scene. Now, they don't share the same enthusiasm about unregulated financial solutions, but lately they've been unable to ignore the size of crypto —or better said, the size of Bitcoin.

So when Dalio says that he appreciates the huge accomplishment of Bitcoin, he's actually referring to it being a potential alternative to cash. In other words, he doesn't so much like Bitcoin as much as he prefers it over the prospect of holding large amounts of cash. And if you think about it, it isn't surprising that he does because US inflation has not been this high since the 1990s. Holding regular cash right now is pretty much an invitation to devaluation, and no investor likes that idea.

There you have it. According to CoinMarketCap, all of crypto currently has a market cap of just over two trillion US dollars, which is no longer a figure mainstream finance can afford to ignore. The market cap of gold is still much higher, at eleven trillion, but that of silver is already at halve crypto's market cap. There is clearly evidence that the cryptoverse is growing fast and nonstop. In view of how poorly fiat money has been doing, it is to be expected that it will continue on that trend, thereby pulling in many other skeptical investors like Dalio.

## ARE BITCOIN AND CRYPTOCURRENCIES A FINANCIAL REVOLUTION?

To answer this question in full, we first need to go back to the fundamental functions of money. Think about it, what properties does money need to have in order to serve its purpose well?

- Money needs to be a unit of account
- It needs to be a store of value
- And it needs to be a means of exchange

Regarding these three basic properties, which you will find listed in almost all definitions of money, crypto is up for debate in at least two of them. It is a unit of account alright, because one Bitcoin plus one Bitcoin equals two Bitcoin. You might be thinking Bitcoin is far too expensive for each unit to be used haphazardly, but then you have smaller portions of it, which are typically nicknamed as Satoshis. So you aspire at having full Bitcoins, but you pay and get paid in Satoshis on a day to day basis. And altcoins are much less expensive, even Ethereum, which is the second most expensive, so crypto can be used as a unit of account without a problem. That much is agreed upon.

As for whether crypto is a reliable store of value, things are harder to decide. For example, people who have profited the most with Bitcoin might argue that it hasn't ever failed them. In reality, though, their very success stories are a testament to how widely Bitcoin's price is likely to change. As I said, it started out being worth less than a dollar back in 2009 and it is now at well over $50,000. No other asset in history has undergone such a radical boost in price, but that in itself doesn't mean Bitcoin is able to store value well. What you want in a currency, fiat or electronic, is for it to be worth more or less the same throughout time. It has to be stable, not change in price. It doesn't matter if it goes up or down, both shifts are undesirable because they interfere with stability.

The counterargument to this could be that all volatility in Bitcoin or other cryptocurrencies is due to a lack of regulation. According to this stance, as soon as things settle down a little and the whole speculative trend reaches a plateau, price stability should become attainable. But do we really want Bitcoin to become stable in price any time soon? An investor should look at opportunities and make the most of them, no matter what they are. In this case, Bitcoin's price volatility is something no one could have predicted, but regardless we should embrace it and profit from it while it's possible.

In short, as of yet it can't be said that any cryptocurrency is a proper store of value. Although they are equipped to work as money and they are often used as such, their price is unstable. You can resort stablecoins to get price stability without resorting to fiat currency, but at that point you're not using crypto as it was originally intended.

If all of this wasn't enough, the final question is even more complex. I guess you've probably heard of non-fungible tokens (NFTs). The reason they're called non-fungible is they aren't interchangeable like you would expect with regular currencies. For example, let's say you have a one dollar bill and I have a one dollar bill. Quite logically, neither of us should see any problem in switching our bills, right? What matters is the value indicated in the bill, not the bill itself.

This is very important for money because it guarantees you can both pay and get paid without wondering where the money came from. All you need to care about is that it's the right amount—period. That means money is fungible. But crypto isn't like that. Every new coin that is created by the blockchain has a distinctive identification number. Well, in all honesty, so do one dollar bills, but no one's really keeping track of those numbers, whereas with crypto, they do. People know which crypto coin is which, whence it came from and where it went. In the world of crypto, it is perfectly possible to track down every single coin, so although we're anonymous, the history of our coins can give us away.

Now, why should this matter if we don't really have anything to hide? Shouldn't we be able to worry about our transparent purchases alone and let the rest get in trouble if they want? Sure, ideally, that should be how things work, but things aren't that simple. For example, imagine what would happen if you were to exchange a bit of ETH with someone else's Bitcoin. You know your ETH hasn't been tampered with because you're an honest person, and that's alright. But what about the Bitcoin you're receiving? How can you know for sure that the person who's giving it to you hasn't used it for anything illegal? Or how can you know they themselves didn't get it from someone else who definitely did? All these questions are virtually impossible to answer.

But in the cryptoverse, they matter more than you'd think. Since every coin is traceable, you might very well ignore whether you're getting paid with untampered Bitcoin, but the authorities won't be so indifferent about it. So that's the problem with crypto not being fungible as regular fiat currencies. You yourself aren't responsible for where a particular coin may come from, but it is still going to be stained, as it were, and the authorities will know.

Certain altcoins are designed to address this very problem, like Monero and Pirate Coin. With these privacy coins, fungibility is possible by cloaking both your ID and that of the coins themselves. That way you do get total anonymity and you don't need to worry about the origin of your coins. But this isn't something we find in all cryptocurrencies. Moreover, those that are most well-known all tend to be non-fungible.

- A brief digression

The flipside to all of this is the existence of NFTs, which have truly taken an unexpected path in relation to crypto as a whole. The same property that keeps crypto from being a convenient fungible currency like regular money is what makes NFTs possible. As I'm sure you know, the latter have been used lately to enable new forms of digital artwork because they solve an old issue we used to have. With all forms of digital files, copying them is as simple as pressing command-c and command-v. There is no sense of originality as such because no single file can be kept from being reproduced.

Of course, this caused the digital world to be rather unfriendly to any form of intellectual or artistic property. Your having a file doesn't prevent me from having an exact copy of it if I want to, so

75

what would be the point of buying digital artwork in the first place? Well, NFTs are non-fungible, just like crypto, so they provide a tool to prevent the reproduction of digital files. That way artists can sell or auction their artwork solely through digital means. Their artwork itself can still be unique even if it doesn't exist physically, so they have a way to monetize it that didn't exist before.

———

Regardless, it must be said that cryptocurrencies clearly lack the fungibility and the price stability that regular money has. Undoubtedly they have brought a new way of decentralized financial systems, they allow people to dispense with banks and transfer money directly amongst one another. At the same time, these key differences that have just been discussed have prevented crypto from truly displacing fiat currency as the central means of payment. It will certainly be present in the future, but the changes that it suffers will probably go along those lines too.

All in all, can it be said that crypto has revolutionized finance? Absolutely. Is it realistic to expect it to change a whole lot more in the near future? Again, absolutely. For us, though, who wish to use it as a means of investment, there is no need to wait for those changes to come. Crypto's appearance has brought with it a very unique window of opportunity. Some people are only just starting to take notice, but fortunately this window is likely to stay open for a good while yet. You can be positive that learning about crypto is one of the wisest investments you can make. You just need to be aware that there's no such thing as learning this once; you must keep updating your knowledge with every day that goes by.

## SOME IMPORTANT MILESTONES

As a kind of trivia trip down memory lane, it's helpful to go over some of the most notable milestones in crypto's history. First when Bitcoin was created and led the way for most innovations, to the point where Ethereum came around and introduced a whole new set of innovations on top of Bitcoin's. These two are arguably the most prominent cryptocurrencies to date, and it's not because of their price but because of their sheer contribution to crypto's launch and improvement. If it weren't for them, crypto would still be nothing more than a good idea sitting around in an academic white paper. But anyway, let's see what we must know to be well learned in the field of crypto.

- October 2008: Bitcoin's creation

Satoshi released their now world famous white paper explaining, from a highly technical standpoint, the ins and outs of their new proposed form of electronic money. It's the kind of document you only want to read if you are familiar with some basic computer science, cryptography and economics, so keep in mind it's not intended for the regular public. At any rate, Satoshi states in it from the very beginning that having a third party monitoring payments defeats the purpose of having passcodes (Satoshi, 2008). This is an idea that has still kept very much alive in the spirit of all other cryptocurrencies in existence. Clearly, although many have pointed out how Bitcoin can be improved, everyone seems to agree on what it did just right.

- January 2009: The genesis block

The very first block in Bitcoin's blockchain is the block zero, which includes 50 Bitcoins that cannot be spent or reused in any way by future transactions. It is a block in which Satoshi themselves participated and it's famous for including a quote from a newspaper headline, as I said earlier in the book. The headline shows the spirit in which Bitcoin was created, one of criticism of the 2008 financial recession. Other than that, we know that Satoshi released one of their last emails right around the time of creating the genesis block. In it, they released the Bitcoin software for everyone to download and start mining on their own.

- May 2010: The world's most expensive pizza

Laszlo Hanyecz bought two Papa John's pizzas for him and his kids at a price of 10,000 Bitcoin. At the time, this much of the cryptocurrency wasn't worth any more than $25. Little did Haniecz know that what he spent on these pizzas would quickly become a fortune he would regret having wasted so gratuitously. The price he paid for the pizzas is now worth a little less than $600 million. To be fair, there really wasn't any clear sign back then that Bitcoin would undergo such a steep upward price shift. Either way, the fact remains that whoever got paid that amount, if they were wise enough to keep it, is now very rich.

- February 2011: Silkroad and its nefarious consequences

Young Ross Ulbricht created a website called Silkroad, supposedly to enable free speech and trade, but which ultimately ended up helping criminal activity through the internet. Silkroad became famous for allowing payments made with Bitcoin, which back in those years was still a pretty uncommon thing. The problem is this quickly became a vehicle for reprehensible trade. Two years later, in 2013, the site was shut down, all Bitcoin was confiscated and sold by the US government, and Ulbricht was imprisoned. Later in 2015, he was given two consecutive life sentences, which some have argued is too hard. In any case, Ulbricht found himself at the center of a hot topic, cybercrime, so his case helped bring wide attention over the potential risks of Bitcoin.

- January 2014: Mt. Gox opens the path for regulation

Along the same line, Japanese crypto exchange Mt. Gox was hacked around the same time. I already mentioned this case, but what I didn't say is that the then CEO of the exchange, Mark Karpeles, was also tried for negligent management (McMillan, 2014). In this case, Karpeles was undoubtedly not diligently doing his job, so the hacking episode may have been avoided, had he been more responsible. He didn't suffer such severe consequences as Ulbricht, but like him, Karpeles contributed to the start of Bitcoin's bad fame. The years 2013 to 2014 were arguably the start of a long list of infamous episodes that drove people to doubt Bitcoin and focus more on its risks than on the possibilities that it offered.

- 2015: Ethereum's creation

Young Vitalik Buterin, staunch Bitcoin advocate though he was, came up with some of the first ideas on how to improve it. He and the team that eventually went on to create Ethereum invented at least two great ideas that are still very much en vogue today, ICOs and smart contracts. ICOs are a method of crowdfunding that is done on the Ethereum platform and over time has allowed for many other altcoins to garner the resources for their own venture. At times, this has also opened the door to scammery, but in essence the idea is just brilliant and generous as can be. This is in part possible due to Ethereum's second great invention, smart contracts, which hold crowd funds without the need of a third party so we get the best of both worlds: people can still organize large projects with crowdsourced funds and still dispense with central monitoring authorities.

- June 2016: The DAO gets hacked

As I just mentioned, Ethereum's tremendously successful crowdfunding method, not surprisingly, was hacked. Most notably, the DAO hack was the time that its Decentralized Autonomous Organization (DAO) was more or less copied by a fake version counterfeited by a hacker. The episode took place back when Ethereum was only worth some $20 per unit, but still the 3.5 ETH that were stolen amounted to a lot of money and a lot of controversy to top it off. It is an issue that has since been addressed, but it pointed to one of crypto's main weaknesses: the fact that although legitimate means of funding a project, ICOs are sometimes seen as too risky to get into.

———

Although there are surely many more memorable milestones to recount, we leave the list as is to move on and cover a question that is perhaps more important for us. What does the future hold for Bitcoin and crypto in general? How will they keep evolving over time? And above all, how should we prepare for things to come? These are some of the questions that we'll cover in the following chapter.

## CHAPTER SUMMARY

- As of the present, crypto is a unit of account, but it isn't a store of value and therefore neither is it a proper means of exchange.
- Crypto is non-fungible, so each individual coin can be traced. This is detrimental to the prospects of crypto as a form of money, but it has interesting applications, like NFTs.
- Some of crypto's milestones: Bitcoin's creation (2008), the genesis block (2009), Ethereum's creation (2015). All other relevant news and scandals have contributed to crypto, both for fame and criticism.

# CHAPTER 8
# HOW WILL CRYPTO CHANGE, IF AT ALL?

Perhaps two of the biggest unknowns when asking this question are these:

- Energy efficiency
- CBDCs

If the future of crypto is to be found anywhere in the present, it may come down to these things. First, how crypto will solve its logistic problems, fundamentally how it will reduce electricity consumption as it continues to grow. Secondly, how governments around the world will react to this continued growth and whether their own initiative, CBDCs, will have a major impact in the world of crypto. Therefore let's take a closer look at each of these subjects.

- Crypto's electricity consumption

On the one hand, Bitcoin hasn't done anything but increase its energy consumption and it is uncertain whether it will stop at any point. As I mentioned earlier, it started out eating up the same energy consumption of small countries like Ireland, and it is now comparable to bigger countries, like Thailand or France. On the other hand, there is a lot of talk around how the Proof of Stake protocol will enhance the energy consumption of several other altcoins (Cooling, 2021), like Tezos, Polkadot, Cardano and Ethereum. In all honesty, I think even the PoS protocol will probably require some fine tuning before it gets to the sweet spot where it is both efficient and flexible to expand.

This is an aspect that will certainly play a big role in the future of crypto. There are big reasons to be excited about PoS and how it will change the game, not just for crypto but even for tech as a whole. If we think about it, the electric car industry faces similar problems right now. Everyone knows or agrees that electric vehicles have to be accessible worldwide in order to overcome climate change, but the logistics are difficult to tackle. Once the techniques are already there, producing enough electric vehicles for the entire planet then becomes fundamentally a logistics problem. Likewise, imagining a world where every single person has at least one crypto wallet is a logistic problem. It would certainly bloat energy consumption even more than it has up till now, and there is great need for innovative ideas in this area.

But there is a flipside to this. In real terms, and for all its wasteful infrastructure, Bitcoin's electricity cost amounts to just 0.1% of the entire world's electricity consumption (Rosenberg, 2021). In other words, comparing this Bitcoin's consumption with that of other countries can be both illustrative and misleading. You get a comparison like that and you will immediately think: "Oh my god, that's a lot." But if you take that information and put it on par with other similar industries, you get a different outcome. Google, for instance, was much more wasteful than Bitcoin every single year since 2015. The question is, though, do people feel the same way about Google than they feel about Bitcoin? In other words, which of the two is wasteful and which isn't, and should we go about figuring that out?

First of all, it would perhaps help pointing out that Bitcoin's electricity consumption is neither unsustainable nor higher than everything we've seen before. So, if people question the electricity cost of bitcoin, this isn't because data is there to back their position. It is mainly because they fail to see it as a necessary expense. Now, that's a far better way of looking at things. Just like with any regular investment in life, what makes an expense justifiable and "not wasteful" is that people see it as such and agree with the purpose it serves. As of now, Bitcoin doesn't have that and it is debatable whether other cryptocurrencies will be met with a different outcome.

Or is it? You see, while there are still many (in fact most) people who haven't yet tried Bitcoin or any other cryptocurrency, those of us who did try it—well, we love it. It offers something no other form of national money has ever been able to give people. It gives you privacy, it gives you state of the art tech, and it gives you freedom to spend indistinctly no matter where you are in the world. Granted, there are countries that have banned it and it may never get full recognition. However, almost all countries have some informal channel through which crypto is still usable. You just need to know where to look. So the real question then is, those who have tried this kind of freedom and know it first hand, how can we ever give it up for lesser alternatives?

My belief is that if you give it enough time, decentralized crypto will manage to earn a place in everybody's hearts. It may seem hard to believe now that there's so much talk about crypto bans and whatnot. But believe me. The future of money is electronic, for sure, and decentralized crypto will certainly play a big role in that future.

- CBDCs Vs. decentralized cryptocurrencies

However, decentralized crypto now also faces a serious challenger, one that we already discussed a while ago: central bank digital currencies. These are, in a way, much more akin to the concept of stablecoins than to cryptocurrencies, to be honest. Yes they are going to be electronic, but the whole spirit of freedom gets lost in them. Their purpose isn't giving you and me a borderless kind of money, but to monetize on one of the biggest commodities of the modern era: information.

Here's how it goes. CBDCs are an attempt at doing what Facebook did a while ago, although Facebook did it ultimately to fail. Have you heard the news on this? Back in 2019, Facebook announced its plans to launch an international cryptocurrency called Libra (Hecker, 2021). The plan was intended to have worldwide reach, and come to think of it, it isn't surprising why Facebook wanted to do it. Their whole profitability relies on user data that they can sell to advertisers, so just imagine: how much data do you think you could get from tracing the use of a cryptocurrency? When we talk about Bitcoin or other decentralized cryptocurrencies, all this data of course goes nowhere. There is no company or government that can build its business model around it, which is why advocates defend them.

In the end, Libra didn't succeed. Governments were quick to understand that their citizen's data was something too valuable for them to give up to a private company. Which is not to say, of course, that they didn't intend to take advantage of it themselves, and this is how we finally arrive at CBDCs.

The potential advantages of monitoring the use of money on a 24/7 basis are huge. It's not exactly as though governments would use this data like advertisers, but they could study and understand their own economies much better. They would get a close look at something that before they could only study indirectly. Because of this change, monetary policy would probably act on a more informed basis and it might also take on an appearance that we haven't yet seen in previous history. Now, all of this sounds truly fascinating, but that is not at all the same as saying that it's good news. Put very simply, the very spirit with which Bitcoin was created would end up being used for the exact opposite purpose.

Another huge consequence CBDCs would bring on the table is, as I mentioned earlier, the disappearance of private or so-called narrow banking. This is because a bank's primary function is creating money through the issuance of credit to the public. But if credit starts being extended directly from central banks, there would no longer be a need for this middle step. This of course would make things much more practical and easy for central banks, and ultimately for governments. However, it would also increase their monitoring of our every move, which means the importance of decentralized cryptocurrency will almost certainly increase in the near future.

## SCALABILITY, USABILITY AND VOLATILITY

Beyond these two central aspects there are others that will still play a decisive role. I'm referring in this case to crypto's ability to scale up its payment processing speed, also to whether it will turn into a standard in the world of money, and finally whether it will ever become stable in terms of its price. These are all things people have been discussing for quite some time now, and there are even some ideas as to how to solve them.

- Scalability

Some people argue that actually this is *the* most important challenge to Bitcoin, and there is some truth to that stance. Quite simply, the problem is that some cryptocurrencies having grown so large and in such little time, it often takes transactions a few minutes, if not up to an hour, to be processed. You may be wondering why that is such a big deal, and the problem is other payment processors, like Visa, are much faster. Visa can take care of around 1,600 transactions per second and up to 150 million in a whole day (Vermeulen, 2017). By contrast, Bitcoin can only process 7 transactions in each block and every block can take between ten minutes and an entire hour to be processed. This means that Bitcoin is immensely slower than regular payment processors.

Some other cryptocurrencies have tried to improve in this area. For example, Litecoin can process up to 56 transactions per second and

Ethereum up to 25 (Newbery, 2021). Still, there is doubtless a long way to go yet. It's not just that by comparison Visa is much faster. It's that in order for exchanges to be competitive for intensive investment activity, they must be quick and regularly updated. Now, there are some altcoins that have really caught up with regular payment processing speed, like Monero, Ripple and Solana, but these are niche products. They are widely used within the cryptoverse, but for the wider audience to notice the difference, these changes must probably happen to one of the major cryptocurrencies that everyone knows and loves.

- Usability

The limited reach of Bitcoin is, in some ways, hard to imagine because of how much it makes the headlines lately. Not a single day goes by without some breaking, entertaining news piece about crypto. After only a decade, it has really turned into a subject that is in everyone's mouth. But does this popularity translate into actual usability? Is there a significant part of the world population actively using crypto in their day to day life?

This could remind us of the early days of the internet, back when connecting to a modem was a complex operation very few would venture into. Nowadays it's so natural that we rarely think of how strange the internet was to people. Today, likewise, buying or selling Bitcoin or another cryptocurrency, creating crypto wallets to store money or participating in ICOs is by no means designed for all audiences. There are some who clearly feel more enthusiastic than the rest.

But I believe things are already well poised to achieve radical change in this area. The cryptoverse has been receiving a favorable tailwind since at least 2017 and since then it hasn't stopped being in people's heads. The non-savvy still feel very intimidated by the very subject, but even those kinds of people can't help but feel curious. Provided enough user experience matters are discussed, the ways in which we use crypto will become even more friendly than they are today. As this change continues to happen, usability and normality will surely increase as well.

- Volatility

Since they cannot as yet hold value in a stable manner, we know by now that cryptocurrencies aren't to be considered currencies in the full sense of the word. As an example, we need only look at Bitcoin's price history and we'll appreciate how extraordinary, but unlike money its trajectory has been. But as I said in the beginning of this book, Bitcoin also has a limited supply of 21 million, a number it hasn't reached yet but that is getting closer and closer every year. Other altcoins also have similar properties in this regard. So although crypto's price is highly volatile right now, expect to see big changes around this in the not too distant future.

After just a single decade, it can't really be said that crypto is an old thing. Thus one of its most prized qualities, scarcity, is something we haven't gotten to experience completely yet. So far, the only thing we have experienced is that the trickle down supply of a deflationary currency causes a severe effect in price stability. In the face of strong shifts in demand, whether up or down, the price too suffers big, sudden changes.

Many have argued this is the primary problem Bitcoin needs to solve, and by extension so do other cryptocurrencies. However, I think this isn't so much a problem to solve as much as a situation that will pass. All existing cryptocurrencies are still for now going through an issuance period. Those that have a fixed supply limit, like Bitcoin, will not be in that phase forever. Eventually, it is to be expected that they will become more stable.

For the time being, and while this process is still unfolding before us, you just need to worry about two things. First, that you take advantage of crypto's price shifts while at the same time taking care of not having a mere FOMO attitude. Secondly, that in the meantime you make your profit by embarking on the crypto wagon, but park your wealth on stablecoins or other similarly stable stores of value.

———

Summing up, the future of crypto and how it will continue to evolve is very uncertain, but we can get a ballpark by looking at current controversial topics. I would argue that the two most decisive are crypto's electricity consumption and also its most fierce rival, CBDCs. But there are also other surrounding unknowns that are closely related to the previous two. The much debated questions of crypto's scalability, usability and volatility all point to key areas of improvement around the original Bitcoin design.

The current scenario provides numerous opportunities for profit for the well informed investor. Mind you, it would be deceitful to go at it expecting to find a magic chest. This is in fact the very reason why so many have tried and failed. But you know very well by now that crypto is not that different from other forms of investment. You can research it, study it carefully and make decisions with that information backing you up. If you do this, you will have very high chances of thriving as a crypto investor.

## CHAPTER SUMMARY

- The two crucial questions to how crypto will continue to evolve: energy efficiency and CBDCs.
- Crypto's energy consumption is comparable to that of midsize countries, but still amounts to just 0.1% of the world's entire energy consumption. Crypto also uses less electricity than Google.
- The latest improvement in this area is the new Proof of Stake protocol, which has shown encouraging results in several well-known altcoins.
- The real question is whether people consider crypto's energy usage justifiable.
- CBDCs, crypto's strongest contender, are interested in the power of money data. It is unlikely that they will crush decentralized crypto, but their impact is going to be huge.
- Crypto's three other questions for the future: scalability, usability and volatility.
- Crypto needs to improve its payment processing speed in order to meet the world's demands.
- Crypto needs to become more friendly to uninitiated users.
- Crypto needs to solve its price volatility issues if it is to be trusted and used as a realistic form of money.

# CHAPTER 9
# SOME BASIC INVESTMENT STRATEGIES FOR THE UNINITIATED

Aside from using staking and mining as a means to have some passive income on the side, there are several other alternatives you have in the world of crypto. Not only that, looking for alternatives is a very wise idea since mining and staking are likely to plateau in terms of the people who are allowed to do it. The truth is they're technically challenging investments and there isn't even a guarantee that they will be profitable in the end. So what are the alternatives?

Before we sink our teeth into them, you must take on this from an information theory standpoint. By this I mean to say that crypto is 100% an internet phenomenon, so it's very much subject to online popular opinion. As you probably know, the first crypto boom occurred back in 2017 (North, 2018), which is the year that it had a whopping 2000% increase in value. When this occurred, crypto was defined by old fashioned investors as "a fraud worse than tulip bulbs," which alluded to a similar craze around tulips back in the 17th century. Now, this kind of prejudice may very well have been proven wrong by now, but regardless, many amanteur investors run to crypto back in 2017.

As a consequence, crypto has arguably become speculative ground even more than in the pre 2017 era. The reason is that amateur investors don't really follow discipline when it comes to decision making. Instead, they follow their instincts, their friends' advice or the latest tabloid news. In other words, they follow an impulse we all have, but they fail to see how that impulse will ever reach an actual end. So that's one of the pitfalls you want to avoid, the rushed enthusiasm of wanting to participate at all costs.

The other big prejudice, however, has to do with the people who called crypto a "fraud." By contrast, those who agree with that opinion are generally trained investors. They feel they know their ground and that they don't need anything new under the sky to keep outperforming the markets. In all fairness, they are right in being prudent, but they're simply wrong in judging crypto without actually having taken the time to know it. In their own way, they too are acting without the proper well informed foundation that a competent crypto investor wishes to have. So again, this is the other big pitfall you want to avoid. To make a profit with crypto, you should neither launch towards it without a plan, nor withhold because you fear it may be just a scam.

- Hodl

And luckily for you, there are also different degrees of adventure you can choose from when investing in crypto. For starters, and this is something I mentioned earlier, you can just buy crypto and hold on to it.

You probably know how the story goes, but I'll tell it just to make sure. Back in 2013, a disappointed user posted in a Bitcoin forum that they had decided to hold their crypto because, and this was the lesson that caused such appraisal, "traders can only take your money if you sell" (Nguyen, 2019). But this user posted their ranting point of view, amidst one of Bitcoin's falls, with a typo: they wrote "hodl" instead of "hold."

Needless to say, the typo has been circling the globe ever since and has actually become somewhat of a battle cry amongst crypto enthusiasts. You see, the philosophy behind it is quite sound and insightful. The theory here is that if you just don't sell there is only so much that you can lose, whereas in selling you buy yourself out of unforeseeable profits. This of course may have sounded like just another disappointed ranting back in 2013, but now that we all know what happened in the following years—well, let's just say everyone now agrees that hodling is the way to go.

So if you're still too nervous about crypto and feel you'd just make mistakes if you were to indulge in it, hodling could be the ideal solution for you too. Elaborating a bit, you could, for instance, set aside a small portion of your income every month. I'm talking about a really small percentage, something you won't really miss if you end up losing. Let's say you set aside 5-10% of your income, the amount you would have spent in yoga lessons anyway. You can use that to buy small amounts of crypto and slowly grow your investment without taking any risk even once.

Moreover, you could take two different paths in this plan. You could diversify and buy a different cryptocurrency each month, perhaps following your assessment of the news. On the other hand, you could pick one single cryptocurrency and stick with it until the end. Either way, the goal would be that you don't sell or take any gambles. Instead, you just wait patiently for those juicy price shifts that crypto is so famous for.

- Futures

The second form of crypto investment is considerably more risky. You shouldn't try it before you feel confident that you have enough experience to understand it and do it correctly. It is an investment method that you'll be somewhat familiar with if you know a thing or two about traditional investment. Put simply, it's a way of making money off crypto without actually owning it yourself, but purchasing derivatives instead. Because of this, it is a very popular method among investors who traded in stock markets before, but still feel a bit hesitant about crypto.

In case you haven't heard about derivatives before, they are contracts that enable you to put a stake on a prediction. For example, you can say that the price of a certain asset will go up in the next months, you then stipulate that in the contract. If you end up being right, you get rewarded also according to the agreed upon measure.

As you can imagine, unless you're positive your prediction is correct, there is big room for error in this kind of investment. Yes, you do get crypto exposure without actually having to own it, but you also get high risk exposure to compensate for it. Moreover, investing in futures is usually done with leverage; in other words, with loaned money. This of course adds to the risk.

Imagine you're buying futures on Bitcoin's price and you only have $1,000 to invest with. You may be positive that you're right about your prediction, so you could feel it's a good idea to leverage. That way you can increase your profits in this prediction, albeit with borrowed money. So you get a 5x leverage, say on Binance, and you now have a $5,000 position on that same prediction. In total, you borrowed $4,000.

The idea is that if you could have made a 10% profit, then that percentage is of course bigger as your position increases. With only $1,000 you'd only have made $100, whereas you'd have made $500 with leverage. With sums much bigger than those of our example, you can see how things can look attractive pretty easily. But although this sounds very attractive, it's important to remember that leverage increases both your profits and your losses. If your prediction were wrong, you'd be in trouble because your $1,000 would be taken as collateral and you'd now owe Binance another $4,000.

If you intend to invest in futures, please keep in mind that leverage is highly risky. You are probably better off investing with whatever little money you have at first. Provided your predictions are right, profits will certainly be smaller, but you'll also have peace of mind.

Whether you nail it or fail, you won't incur in debt that you may be unable to pay.

- ICOs

The acronym derives from the mainstream version, initial public offerings (IPOs). These are the events through which companies enter the stock market for the first time and get their stock traded amongst investors for the first time. Similarly, initial coin offerings (ICOs) are a crowdfunding process that was made possible by the Ethereum platform. Through it, new crypto ventures can get access to funding even though they wouldn't be accepted in a traditional stock market.

In terms of structure, the steps a venture has to go through in an ICO are very similar to those of a regular IPO. First, the team gets officially listed in the Ethereum platform to get access to potential investors, and up next they release a prospectus outlining the details of their venture. As an investor, you must read that prospectus very closely, but at the same time, you must find out everything you can about the people involved in it. This way you'll know what kind of project you're funding and you'll also know whether the people behind it are trustworthy.

Although doing these two things is standard procedure no matter what you invest in, it becomes especially important in the context of crypto and ICOs. You see, since there is no SEC or similar regulating authority making sure that scams are screened out of the funding process, it is up to you to look out for risks of this nature. And there are many of them. You may remember just a while ago I told you about the DAO hack. Well, that's an example of this. So you shouldn't freak out and run away with your money, but need to be extra careful, is all.

Moving past that warning, how do you get rewarded when the investment has yielded good results? Quite simply, you get tokens of whatever cryptocurrency you may have funded in the first place. So, for instance, if you had participated in Ethereum's ICO, you'd made a huge profit from it. But the same cannot be said about every altcoin, so in addition to being extra careful, you must be a good picker too.

## CRYPTO EXCHANGES AND BROKERS

You must learn your way through these sites. Brokers are generally going to be much friendlier, and that goes by design, but overall you must aim at being self-sufficient in both arenas. Broadly speaking, brokers are where you go to get a personal, streamlined treatment to help you as you still give your first steps into the crypto world. But in essence, brokers aren't really different from exchanges in any other way. They charge you dearly in exchange for their customized help, but ultimately the service they provide is the same. Exchanges, on the other hand, are the real deal. Almost all the things you can do with crypto, besides sending and receiving it from one user to another, you must do in exchanges. Therefore it's crucial that you:

- Pick the right exchanges
- As I said, withdraw your crypto from their custodial wallets after doing your trading
- Keep alert on fees

Let's start with well-known broker names, like eToro or Plus500. Both of these alternatives have a serious pitfall: they don't let you withdraw your crypto. this can become a problem, say, when you see prices going down. The option to withdraw, or to make most quick moves for that matter, is generally accessible only to advanced services. This is the tradeoff for adding an extra layer to the task. You get help, but you also lose some agility in the response.

Another thing you find in brokers, this time specifically with eToro, is a thing called "communal investing." The idea here is that you get access to the moves more experienced users do, and if you deem them accurate, you get to emulate them with the press of a button. I honestly don't find this to be the ideal way of following advice, but it must be said that it shows you some real life investing. I feel you should make investing decisions on your own, but looking closely at what others do is certainly instructive.

I'm covering brokers briefly because you must be aware of them, and they certainly help during the first steps. However, I think it's best if you're a bit more brave and go directly to exchanges. Although it may seem rather intimidating at first, you would do well to withhold from resorting to brokers. If you really feel the need for qualified help, then you can hire a crypto investor to guide you one on one, or ask your friends for specific advice. Either way, you'll be better off than going to exchanges through the added layer of brokers in the middle.

The best known exchanges are probably Coinbase and Binance, with other slightly smaller examples on the side, like Kraken, KuCoin, FTX or Bitfinex. When I mentioned brokers, I also quoted names that are well-known and guaranteed. So in this case too, whichever exchange you end up choosing, make sure you check it up thoroughly before taking any further steps. For example, take a look at the volume they handle per day. If you visit CoinMarketCap and look up the word "exchanges," you will find a long list displaying that very information along with their overall rating. Binance, for instance, has a trading volume of just under $26 billion per day; Coinbase, almost $6 billion per day. So on and so forth. This number gives you an idea of how legit and active an exchange is, which is important to know.

- Binance and Coinbase compared

Binance, which is available worldwide, offers a form of insurance called Secure Asset Fund For Users (SAFU). This is a very nice tool to have, since we have discussed crypto hacking a number of times. With this option, you basically get some degree of protection against theft. The exchange bundles up 10% of all collected fees in order to create this fund, which can be used to compensate users when they were the victims of a hacking attack.

Another good feature of Binance is that you can open up savings accounts in it. In short, these accounts are just like a custodial wallet, except they give you a small interest return. Provided you have the SAFU option for security, itcan be a good idea to leave some crypto there and let it grow. Of course, exchanges offer these options to encourage users to leave their crypto with them. It's an option to consider, but not one that it'd be bad if you decide you'd rather let it go.

The most obvious area where Coinbase loses in comparison to Binance is the amount of cryptocurrencies they support. Binance supports thousands of them, whereas Coinbase only supports 20. Also, Binance charges a fee of up to 0.1% on your transactions, which is much lower than the 0.5% charged by Coinbase. In fact, Binance has the most competitive fee when compared to rivals.

Coinbase, which is available only in the US, offers you protection from up to $250,000, backed by the FDIC. However, they've also been known to freeze accounts without prior notice, so it's not like you have absolute control over your account, like you would on Binance.

All in all, both Binance and Coinbase offer protection against theft, but only Binance gives you full control. If your interest in crypto goes in hand with autonomy too, I would suggest you pick Binance. Now, of course most users out there usually make use of more than one exchange. At any rate, keep in mind that most reviewers and commentators agree that Binance is probably the best overall contender for now.

# CHAPTER SUMMARY

- Crypto is an internet phenomenon, so in absence of regulation, the primary force that pushes it around is online public opinion.
- Three ways to invest in crypto, one for each level of risk you feel most comfortable with: simply holding on to it, taking a stake with futures or investing in ICOs.
- Brokers provide a friendly service for the uninitiated, but they're more expensive. Sometimes they will help, but sometimes you'll be better off with individual one on one help, if that's what you want.
- The two biggest exchanges are Binance and Coinbase, the former is available worldwide and the latter only in the US.
- Binance is the overall best exchange because it gives you more security and control over your crypto.

# FINAL WORDS

Whatever may happen to crypto as we know it today, it is certain that we are moving towards a decentralized future. This can be explained by economic reasons of one sort or another, but I believe the key is that crypto, as I said, is an internet phenomenon. And the internet itself is still quite a recent phenomenon, having become widely accessible only since the 80s. Since then, the behavior of businesses and entrepreneurs has never been the same. The promise of the internet was basically what Friedman, an economist we discussed before, had foreseen: that in the near future a new form of decentralized money would overtake the whole financial system and would perhaps even displace governments from their current central role.

Now, if we're going to be realistic about it, Friedman's prediction hasn't really come true, but the public conversation has doubtless veered in that direction. There are new huge companies that didn't exist even as a concept just half a century ago. Think of Google, Amazon, Netflix, Apple or Facebook. All these companies have thrived because they were able to monetize their users database and turn it into a commodity: the oil of the 21st century is data. As a natural consequence, we have seen a big trend in people wanting to withdraw to an open, decentralized environment where their data isn't monitored.

Just like it may happen to crypto in view of CBDCs, the original spirit of the internet too has been largely diverted. The internet was intended to be a decentralized network for people across the world to exchange information in a free and highly efficient manner. This has now been altered in part by the appearance of the big tech companies that I just mentioned, just the most salient examples in a much longer list.

I personally don't subscribe to the libertarian-anarchist trend in crypto advocates, at least not until its most extreme examples. I feel there are several things in crypto that would very much benefit from a little more regulation. But the point here is quite different from saying what each of us stands for. Crypto is a fascinating invention that must surely have been done by qualified, talented people, even if we may never know for sure who they were. It needs improving, no doubt, and it will get it from those who don't just focus on fearing it or adoring it without limit. It will continue to surprise people all around the world as modern national electronic money continues to become more and more centralized.

The possibility we enjoy right now of having thousands of developers around the world improving upon the open source software is just something priceless. Any other manner of undertaking these projects, under private or government watch, would cost millions. With crypto, it is all done out of a spirit for profit, but also to make crypto as best as it can be.

The economy of crypto, which is still in the making, already enables people to enjoy a series of possibilities they didn't have before. Decentralization, as I began by saying, is quite simply here to stay. In the coming years, it will doubtless keep reducing the role of governments and large multinationals, and in that promise it will bring back the original spirit of the internet itself. While these changes take place, you must sail knowing that there is nothing as risky as constantly changing scenes. There is still a lot to keep alert for, and I hope to have given you the tools to be on the watch on your own from now on.